ARCHAEOLOGY AND BIBLICAL INTERPRETATION

These are exciting times for all those involved in the history of ancient Israel, Judaism and early Christianity, for the last few decades have seen an unprecedented amount of scholarly work upon both textual and artefactual evidence. A clear understanding of the relationship between archaeology and literary material is crucial for scholars who wish to reconstruct the history of emerging Israel.

The papers assembled in this book use the most recent research in key areas – the early settlements of Israel, early Israelite religion, Qumran, Jerusalem, early Christian churches – to show that ancient writings and modern archaeology can illuminate each other, but only when used with professional care. The essays represent a new generation of archaeologists and historians, with new social, political and religious concerns who draw a fresh and vital picture of the emergence of ancient Israel.

John R. Bartlett is the Principal of the Church of Ireland Theological College. He has researched and published widely in the history and archaeology of ancient Moab and Edom. He is the author of *Edom and the Edomites* (1990) and *The Bible: Faith and Evidence* (1990).

ARCHAEOLOGY AND BIBLICAL INTERPRETATION

Edited by John R. Bartlett

London and New York

First published 1997
by Routledge
11 New Fetter Lane, London EC4P 4EE

Simultaneously published in the USA and Canada
by Routledge
29 West 35th Street, New York, NY 10001

selection and editorial matter © 1997 John R. Bartlett
individual chapters © 1997 the contributors

Typeset in Garamond by Florencetype Ltd, Stoodleigh, Devon

Printed and bound in Great Britain by
Biddles Ltd, Guildford and King's Lynn

British Library Cataloguing in Publication Data

A catalogue record for this book is available from the British Library.

Library of Congress Cataloging in Publication Data

Archaeology and Biblical Interpretation/edited by John R. Bartlett.
Includes bibliographical references and index
1. Bible–Antiquities. 2. Excavations (Archaeology)–Middle East.
3. Bible–Criticism, interpretation, etc.
4. Bible–Evidences, authority, etc.
5. Middle East–Antiquities. I. Bartlett, John R. (John Raymond)
BS621.A68 1996
220.9'3–dc20   96-13808
ISBN 0-415-14113-3 (hbk)
ISBN 0-415-14114-1 (pbk)

CONTENTS

FIGURES

CONTRIBUTORS

John R. Bartlett was formerly Associate Professor of Biblical Studies, Trinity College, Dublin. He is now Principal, Church of Ireland Theological College, Dublin.

Claudine Dauphin is Research Fellow and Professor at the Centre National de la Recherche Scientifique, Paris

William G. Dever is Professor of Near Eastern Archaeology and Anthropology, University of Arizona, Tucson, Arizona.

Sean V. Freyne is Professor of Theology, Trinity College, Dublin.

Brian Lalor was formerly Director of the Architectural Department, Temple Mount Excavations of the Hebrew University/Israel Exploration Society.

Andrew D. H. Mayes is Erasmus Smith's Professor of Hebrew, Trinity College, Dublin.

PREFACE

These papers, with the exception of the last, were first given at colloquia held in Dublin in November 1994 and November 1995 by the Consultative Committee for Biblical and Near Eastern Studies of the Royal Irish Academy. Professor Dauphin's paper was given as a public lecture in Trinity College, Dublin, in February 1995. Their range covers the 'biblical period' and the early Christian period, but, more importantly, these papers are each focused on one of the major debates of current concern in the history of ancient Israel and early Christianity.

Given the large number of popular works on the Bible that make simplistic and often misleading use of archaeological material, the complex relationship of textual and archaeological evidence is high on the present agenda. The editor's opening essay explores the issues involved. Clear understanding of this relationship is particularly important for scholarly attempts to reconstruct the history of emergent Israel; it is now increasingly clear that the primary evidence is archaeological, and that the value of the biblical narratives of the entry to the promised land and the settlement of Canaan need careful evaluation. As a practising archaeologist, Professor Dever makes an important contribution to the evidence for this re-evaluation (chapter 2).

A related subject which has come into its own in recent years is the religion of early Israel. The artefactual evidence for religious practices in the land of Israel in the early first millennium BCE has been greatly increased by the surge of recent excavation in Israel and elsewhere, and this material sets the presentation of Israel's religion by the Deuteronomist and other biblical writers in a new light. In chapter 3 Professor Mayes, well known for his work on the early history of Israel, discusses the graffiti from Kuntillet 'Ajrud, an Iron Age caravanserai on the route to Egypt, with their alleged references to a female consort for the Israelite god Yahweh, and assigns to them an historical context in the development of Israel's religion.

From the Second Temple period of Israel's history, the Dead Sea Scrolls have been much in the news as scholars have succeeded in bringing to the light of publication a number of documents first discovered in the 1950s. The relationship of the site of Qumran to the scrolls found in caves nearby has come under new scrutiny, and the long-established view of the site as a kind of ancient monastery has been vigorously challenged. In chapter 4 the editor examines these recent views in the light of the archaeological evidence. Since 1967, the area of the Temple Mount in Jerusalem has been the object of intensive research, exploration and excavation, and an up-to-date, comprehensive study is urgently required. Brian Lalor applies his architectural skills and experience in Jerusalem to presenting the archaeological and literary evidence in chapter 5.

Again, the quest for the Jesus of history has taken a new turn in the last decade, with new emphasis on the social context of the first century, and Professor Freyne, well known for his work on Jesus and Galilee, brings us up to date in chapter 6. And, lastly, much work has been done in recent years on the archaeology and history of both Jewish and Christian places of worship, synagogues and churches, in the early centuries of the present era; Professor Dauphin presents the results of her excavation of the Byzantine basilica (built over a Hellenistic temple) at Dor.

These are exciting times for all those involved in the history of ancient Israel, Judaism and early Christianity, for the last few decades have seen an unprecedented amount of scholarly work upon both textual and artefactual evidence. We have never had so many scholarly journals full of new research; we have never seen such co-operation between Jewish, Christian and Islamic scholars; there has never before been such a wide and receptive audience of informed members of the public anxious to hear and read more. The last thirty years have seen the development of a completely new approach to this area of history. This new approach has been influenced on the one hand by the development of the social sciences, and on the other by the new availability of a wealth of archaeological data throwing perhaps more light on the social context and the working world of ancient Israel than on military and political aspects. One might add that a new, younger generation of archaeologists and historians, with new social, political and religious concerns, has seen ancient Israel and early Christianity through different eyes, and has presented a fresh and vital new picture; and this has important implications for the theologians also, whose work must, if it is to be honest, take account of biblical and historical scholarship. This collection of papers from Dublin is one small contribution to the larger process.

John R. Bartlett.
Dublin, April 1996

ABBREVIATIONS

AB	*Anchor Bible*
ABD	*Anchor Bible Dictionary*
Annales	*Annales. Economies, sociétés, civilisations*
ARW	*Archiv für Religionswissenschaft*
ASOR	*American Schools of Oriental Research*
ASORDS	American Schools of Oriental Research Dissertation Series
BA	*Biblical Archaeologist*
BAIAS	*Bulletin of the Anglo-Israel Archaeological Society*
BAR	British Archaeological Reports International Series
BARev	*Biblical Archaeology Review*
BASOR	*Bulletin of the American Schools of Oriental Research*
Bib	*Biblica*
B Z	*Biblische Zeitschrift*
BTAVO	Beihefte zum Tübinger Atlas des Vorderen Orients
BThB	*Biblical Theology Bulletin*
CSSH	Comparative Studies in Society and History
EI	*Eretz-Israel*
ESI	*Excavations and Surveys in Israel*
FRLANT	Forschungen zur Literatur des Alten und Neuen Testaments
HTR	*Harvard Theological Review*
IEJ	*Israel Exploration Journal*
ILN	*Illustrated London News*
INJ	*Israel Numismatic Journal*
JBL	*Journal of Biblical Literature*
JFA	*Journal of Field Archaeology*
JNES	*Journal of Near Eastern Studies*
JR	*Journal of Religion*

JRA	*Journal of Religion in Africa*
JSJ	*Journal for the Study of Judaism*
JSOT	*Journal for the Study of the Old Testament*
JSPSup	*Journal for the Study of the Pseudepigrapha Series Supplement*
MT	Masoretic Text
NTS	*New Testament Studies*
PEFQS	*Palestine Exploration Fund Quarterly Statement*
PEQ	*Palestine Exploration Quarterly*
RB	*Revue biblique*
RelStRev	*Religious Studies Review*
RevQ	*Revue de Qumran*
SBLASP	Society of Biblical Literature Abstracts and Seminar Papers
SJOT	*Scandinavian Journal of the Old Testament*
TA	*Tel Aviv*
ThR	*Theologische Rundschau*
VT	*Vetus Testamentum*
ZDPV	*Zeitschrift des deutschen Palästina-Vereins*

1

WHAT HAS ARCHAEOLOGY TO DO WITH THE BIBLE – OR VICE VERSA?

John R. Bartlett

INTRODUCTION

I must begin by saying something about the nature of the Bible, and the nature of archaeology, which will at least reveal my starting point. Like all other written books, including other holy books, the Bible is in the first place (whatever value we set upon it) a human artefact, with a human history. It is the product of many different human minds of varying ability, written by human hands of varied powers of co-ordination, copied and recopied by scribes of varied intelligence, printed and bound by craftsmen of varying standards of skill, read and interpreted by Jews and Christians and agnostics and atheists of differing hermeneutical approaches. It is also a book of very varied origins and contents. It is an anthology containing ancient Jewish laws, legends, myths, hymns, songs, love lyrics, proverbs, prophecies, stories, biographies, histories, letters, visions, philosophical reflection and so on, written at different times between, let us say, the eighth century BCE and the early second century of this era. Its many authors wrote to meet the needs of their own times rather than our own. The historians among them wrote history as they saw it, and they presented the past of Israel in terms designed to meet their own political or religious agenda, not our agenda. Divine inspiration may have led them to write better than they knew, but nevertheless they were writing as human beings for their own human situation, and could not have known what use later generations might make of their work or what interpretations they might put on it. And their work is itself part of history, and the historical books of the Bible are part of ancient historiography, to be read and studied alongside other ancient writings and other evidence of that past. And among that 'other' evidence is, of course, what we loosely call 'archaeology'.

'Archaeology' was once a general term referring to study of the past; so Josephus entitled his twenty-volume history of the Jews 'The archaeology of the Jews'. Archaeology now popularly describes the activity of those who excavate ancient sites. The best definition is perhaps that of R. J. Braidwood: 'the study of things men made and did, in order that their whole way of life may be understood' (in *Archaeologists and What They Do* (New York 1960), quoted in Daniel 1967: 17). This is not mere antiquarianism, but an intellectual enquiry into human experience. The professional archaeologist, using a wide range of techniques, studies systematically the material remains of the past and thus contributes to the general historical task along with other scholars who study the literary, inscriptional, artistic or other recorded evidence. The archaeological evidence from the ancient states of Israel and Judah and the ancient writings enshrined in our modern Bible are perhaps the two most important sources for the history of the people of ancient Israel and of the early Christian church; but evidence both archaeological and literary from the ancient surrounding nations – Egypt, Syria, Babylonia, Assyria and the Graeco-Roman world – must not be ignored. Correct assessment of the relative value of evidence from these different sources is the concern of the historian, but correct assessment has always been difficult; the literary scholar has not always understood the limitations of the archaeological evidence, and the archaeologist has not always understood the complexities of the literary evidence. Further, the biblical student and the archaeologist do not always share the same historical aims (let alone theological presuppositions). And some recent scholars would say that archaeology and literary sources simply do not meet, and cannot be synthesised; they are like apples and oranges, two completely different species. Axel Knauf argues that you have to know the history (from artefactual sources) before you can interpret the documents (1991: 26–64); T. L. Thompson argues that you have to establish an independent narrative of ancient Palestine as the context from which the text might speak (1991: 65–92); while J. M. Miller argues contrarily that you cannot interpret the artefacts without the written sources (1991: 93–102). The struggle continues, and we will return to it.

DEVELOPMENT OF ARCHAEOLOGY IN RELATION TO BIBLICAL STUDIES

It is in fact hard to say when archaeological observation relating to biblical material began. For example, the ancient writer who noted the contemporary ruins of the ancient city of Ai (Josh 8:28) had an archaeologist's eye. So perhaps did Helena, wife of the emperor Constantine, who in 326 CE visited Palestine and founded basilicas at sites associated with Christ's life and death (but for her motivation, see Hunt 1982: 22–49), and the Bordeaux Pilgrim, who in 333 CE distinguished between the modern Jericho and the earlier city of Jericho by Elisha's fountain (Wilkinson 1971: 153–63 [160–1]). From the Byzantine age to the time of the Crusades, most western travellers to the Holy Land were pilgrims, interested in locating places associated with Christ or other famous biblical figures. Particularly important were the early fourth-century onomastikon of Eusebius (a gazetteer of biblical place names), the early fifth-century travelogue of the Spanish nun Egeria (Wilkinson 1971: 89–147), a mine of topographical information, and the sixth-century mosaic map of the Holy Land on the floor of a church in Madeba, east of the Dead Sea (Jenkins 1930; Avi-Yonah 1954; Wilken 1992: 174–81). These all reveal minds that were not simply pietistic; whatever the travellers' motivations, it will not do to deny the presence of academic observation before the Renaissance (Peters 1985; Wilkinson 1977). The tenth-century Islamic scholar, Mukaddasi, and the late twelfth-century Jewish rabbi, Benjamin of Tudela in Spain, and others, explored and described Palestine with critical eyes, but their works were not known in the west, and so did not influence western scholarship, until much later. The Crusades renewed western interest in the geography and topography of the Holy Land, at least among the participants and pilgrims who followed in their wake; such pilgrims did not travel as archaeologists, but their writings frequently show that they were not unobservant or without concern for historical detail (see, for example, North 1979: 93–110).

A whole series of papers might be written about the development of western intellectual and scientific interest in the Holy Land from the Crusades to the nineteenth century, and about the progression of travellers, some more curious and discerning than others, who began to observe and report the material remains of earlier ages, but that is not our object here. The nineteenth century is a major study in itself (cf. Ben-Arieh 1979), but there is no time to pursue it in this paper. The nineteenth century saw the dramatic expansion of archaeological and biblical study. This expansion owed much to political and economic factors such as the quest for a land route from the eastern Mediterranean to India, the imperial designs of Napoleon (whose surveyors mapped Palestine), the arrival of the steam ship and the steam locomotive, the development of photography and of a cheaper printing technology, and the growth of education for all. In an era when the Protestant churches set a high premium on biblical knowledge and Sunday Schools flourished, there was increasing interest in biblical geography, biblical peoples and their customs, and a ready market for the hundreds of books, especially illustrated books, published on Palestinian travel (see Searight 1979; Ben-Arieh 1979; Silberman 1982; North 1979).

Probably the most important contribution for biblical scholars and archaeologists alike was Edward Robinson's *Biblical Researches in Palestine* (1841, 1856). With Eli Smith, a Protestant missionary and fluent Arabist, Robinson travelled the length and breadth of Palestine in 1838–9 and 1852 in order to locate places mentioned in the Bible. He based many of his identifications on the modern Arabic place-names, which, he argued, preserved the Semitic name from biblical times. Albrecht Alt later commented that 'in Robinson's footnotes are forever buried the errors of many generations' (Alt 1939: 374). Robinson had his limitations – he did not recognise that the tells which dotted the Palestinian plains were not natural hillocks but the remains of city mounds – and he was occasionally wrong, but his work is the foundation of all biblical toponymy and is still an essential reference work.

By 1850 the initial European exploration of Palestine and Transjordan had been achieved; there remained the accurate surveying and the excavation of important biblical sites. First Jerusalem (1865), then Sinai (1868–9), then the whole of western Palestine (1871–7) were surveyed by British army engineers. An important step was the foundation in 1865 of the Palestine Exploration Fund, whose aim was the scientific investigation of 'the Archaeology, Geography, Geology and Natural History of Palestine' (Besant 1886; Watson 1915; cf. *PEQ* 100, 1965: 1–2; Hodson 1993: 6–8). Although at first heavily supported and subscribed to by church leaders, the Fund kept to its scientific aims and flourishes still, especially through its journal, *Palestine Exploration Quarterly*. A younger sister, the British School of Archaeology in Jerusalem, was founded in 1919, modelled on similar schools in Rome and Athens (Auld 1993: 23–6). In France, Germany, America, Israel and elsewhere, similar societies and journals appeared: for example, the first institute of the American Schools of Oriental Research was founded in Jerusalem in 1900 (King 1992: 186–8; 1988: 15–35; 1993: 13–16), followed shortly by its *Bulletin*. In Germany a number of important societies arose, of which the two most important, the Deutsches evangelisches Institut für Altertumswissenschaft des Heiligen Landes (1900) and the Deutscher Verein für Erforschung Palästinas (1877) produced the *Palästina-Jahrbuch* and the *Zeitschrift des deutschen Palästina-Vereins* respectively (Weippert and Weippert 1988: 87–9; Strobel 1993: 17–19). The French Dominicans established the Ecole biblique (1890) and its journal, *Revue biblique*, in 1891 (Benoit 1988: 63–86; Puech 1993: 9–12). In Israel, the Israel Exploration Society (formerly the Jewish Palestine Exploration Society, founded 1914) has produced the *Israel Exploration Journal* from 1951 (Mazar 1988: 109–14).

The first excavation in Palestine was F. de Saulcy's investigation of the 'Tombs of the Kings' in 1863 (Ben-Arieh 1979: 175; Macalister 1925: 26–8). This turned out to be the family tomb of Queen Helena of Adiabene, a first-century convert to Judaism (Prag 1989: 272–4); excavation of a Jewish tomb gave some offence to Jews in Jerusalem. In 1867–8 Charles Warren, RE, dug shafts and tunnels to explore the Herodian temple platform of the Haram area, and he too met some opposition on religious grounds. Sensitivity to the feelings of the present has not always been the first thought of those who explore the past, and it remains important. Warren went on to excavate at Jericho (1868). One notes that the first excavations were directed, quite naturally, at famous biblical cities, and it was largely, though not entirely, the pull of these famous places which set the agenda and helped provide the public contributions which paid for the excavation.

The thing that captured the public imagination and changed the whole perspective on archaeology was the series of astonishing discoveries throughout the nineteenth century in Egypt and Mesopotamia. Scholarly study of Egypt really began with Napoleon's expedition in 1799. Egypt, with its great pyramids and temples, was fun in itself, but for many it was important as the scene of the biblical Exodus, and much scholarly time was given to identifying the 'store cities', Pithom and Ramses, of Exodus 1:12 and to dating the Exodus and identifying 'the Pharaoh of the Exodus' (James 1982). The discovery of the fourteenth-century BCE Amarna Letters, written to the ruling Pharaoh from Canaan, with their reference to the military activity in Palestine of the *habiru*, who sounded suspiciously like the Hebrews, influenced scholarly debate on the date of the Exodus from the 1890s to the 1960s, by which time it was generally accepted that neither the equation of Hebrew with *habiru* nor the nature of the Exodus story was as simple as previously thought (see, for example, Albright 1966: 3–23; Bruce 1967: 3–20; Hayes and Miller

1977: 248–51; Miller and Hayes 1986: 54–79; Coote 1990: 33–93; Na'aman 1992: 174–81).

In Mesopotamia, the identification of Assyrian and Babylonian sites, with their dramatic carved monuments, by explorers and excavators like A. H. Layard (1817–94), and the decipherment of their inscriptions by scholars like Edward Hincks (1792–1866), H. C. Rawlinson (1810–95) and George Smith (1840–76), who discovered a tablet giving an account of a flood remarkably similar to the account in Genesis 6–9, stirred even greater popular enthusiasm. Interest was maintained by Leonard Woolley's claim (1929) to have discovered evidence of the biblical flood at Ur, by the discovery of second-millennium BCE archives at Mari, Nuzi (1925–31) and elsewhere, by the discovery (1911–13) of Hittite records in north-central Turkey, by the discovery (1929) of Canaanite documents at Ras Shamra on the Syrian coast, and by the discovery in 1974 of a huge archive of third-millennium BCE texts from Tell Mardikh (ancient Ebla) in Syria. Such discoveries raised both public and scholarly interest in biblical history; but they illuminated the near-eastern background to the Bible rather than the Bible itself, and are now the concern primarily of specialists in these fields. When exploration of Egypt and Mesopotamia began, Egypt and Mesopotamia were known primarily from the Bible; as Egyptian and Mesopotamian archaeology progressed, Palestine, the land of Israel, began to be seen in the much wider context of the whole near east, and this changed fundamentally the way scholars began to look at ancient Israel. Ancient Israel, and the Bible, became part of a much larger scene.

ARCHAEOLOGY AND BIBLICAL STUDIES IN THE TWENTIETH CENTURY

A new era began with the work of Flinders Petrie at Tell el-Hesi in 1890 (Moorey 1991: 28–9; Drower 1985: 159–63). Petrie discovered from his examination of the mound of Tell el-Hesi, first, that tells were artificial, not natural mounds, formed by the accumulated strata of building debris over long periods of time; and, second, that each visible stratum of deposit contained its own distinctive types of pottery. Petrie produced a classified typology of the pottery taken from the different levels exposed on the mound. This gave a relative dating for the sequence of pottery, which could then be used as an aid to dating similar levels elsewhere in Palestine; the discovery of Egyptian inscriptions or royal scarabs in a stratified context made it possible to link the scheme with the accepted Egyptian chronology and so produce a basic chronology for Palestinian material. The cross-linkage of stratified pottery with Egyptian and Assyrian inscriptional evidence remains vital to the establishment of the chronology of biblical history to this day. Though Petrie was a pioneer, his stratigraphy has not escaped serious criticism (for example Wheeler 1956: 29–34; Davies 1988: 49). Petrie, however, went on to correlate the strata excavated at Tell el-Hesi with the biblical evidence for the history of Lachish (Petrie 1891). This was a dangerous procedure, liable to distort interpretation of the history of the site, for subsequent research has shown that Tell el-Hesi was not Lachish (Doermann 1987: 129–56). The direct association of biblical texts and archaeological evidence has always tempted scholars, and is fraught with risk.

However, stratigraphy and pottery sequences had come to stay. Thirty years later the American scholar W. F. Albright at Tell Beit Mirsim (1926–32) began to refine Petrie's pottery chronology. Albright has been accused of using his knowledge of pottery typology – that is, the observed development of forms of pottery – to determine the stratification of the site, rather than using the observed stratification to determine the pottery typology, and of producing inadequate stratification, but he did construct a new and generally accepted ceramic index for Palestine. His polymathic control of historical and linguistic as well as archaeological data established him as the leading interpreter of biblical history and archaeology in his generation. He valued the evidence of both biblical text and excavated artefacts equally, and thus produced a synthesis which influenced a whole generation of American scholars, in particular biblical scholars and theologians like George Ernest Wright and John Bright, whose books *Biblical Archaeology* (1957) and *A History of Israel* (1960) respectively were standard textbooks for biblical students through the 1960s and 1970s. Albright used this synthesis to support the essential accuracy of the Bible's picture of the patriarchal age, the Exodus and conquest, the period of the Judges and the early monarchy, in opposition to the radical reconstruction of the biblical tradition by German scholars like Wellhausen and Alt and Noth. This synthesis was of course very popular in more conservative quarters, where any archaeological evidence which appeared to give support to the biblical picture was welcomed; but Albright's 'biblical archaeology' synthesis has in turn suffered serious criticism from archaeologists and biblical scholars alike in the last twenty years (see, for example, Moorey 1981: 26–8; 1991: 67–75; Dever 1993: 23–35).

In America, Albright combined the roles of archaeologist and biblical scholar (though his field experience was comparatively limited); in Britain, with rare exceptions, the biblical scholars and archaeologists kept to their separate trades. John Crowfoot, John Garstang, James Starkey, R. W. Hamilton and C. N. Johns were primarily archaeologists, though concerned with biblical history; Kathleen Kenyon studied modern history, and became a protégée of Sir Mortimer Wheeler and, like him, a highly professional archaeologist. Kenyon developed what became known as the Wheeler-Kenyon technique; this used the trench method, but refined it by meticulous observation and recording of the stratigraphy. She checked her stratigraphy by preserving the baulk and drawing its vertical section as a record of what had been dug (Kenyon 1939: 29–37; 1953). Kenyon's excavation of Jericho (1952–9), by careful observation of stratigraphy (see especially Kenyon 1951: 101–38, written before her excavation began), corrected Garstang's dating of his so-called 'double' wall from the Late Bronze to the Early Bronze Age, denied the existence of any but the smallest settlement at Jericho in the Late Bronze Age, and so undermined an influential view of the dating of the Exodus and conquest of Canaan. More importantly in purely archaeological terms, Kenyon revealed at Jericho flourishing Middle Bronze and Early Bronze cities, and a history of the Neolithic period extending back to the tenth millennium BCE (Kenyon 1957). In another major excavation (1961–7) at Jerusalem Kenyon continued the century-old exploration of the topography and history of the city (Kenyon 1974), work continued in the 1970s and 1980s with dramatic success by the Israeli archaeologists Nahman Avigad, Yigael Shiloh, Benjamin Mazar and others. Kenyon was in no way a biblical scholar, and in excavating had no biblical axe to grind. She was concerned to present what the archaeological evidence told her, and took the biblical evidence mostly at face value, without critical analysis; if it fitted, well and good. (For a critique of Kenyon's work, see Moorey 1979: 3–10; Davies 1988: 49–54; Dever 1980: 41–8; Prag 1992: 109–23.) Israeli scholars, understandably, have tended to give greater credence to the biblical traditions and to national history; 'Quite naturally, every opportunity is taken to relate archaeological evidence to the biblical text' (Mazar 1988: 127). In this, as also in their approach to pottery analysis and stratification, they have been closer to the Albright tradition than to the British or German scholarly tradition.

Kenyon was professionally independent of the Bible, and was probably more interested in Neolithic than in biblical material; but she was not quite indifferent to the Bible. In some ways she was part of the era of 'biblical archaeology'; her historical approach reveals the same limitations in scope as does that of her predecessors. For a century the Bible had influenced the choice of sites for excavation, and the aims of the excavators. Concern to establish dates and to verify the biblical presentation of history led to the search for city walls and palaces, temples and their cult vessels, inscriptions and coins; evidence of destruction or cultural change in Palestinian cities at the end of the Late Bronze Age, for example, was promptly related to the biblical account of the Israelite conquest of Canaan, without more ado. This was not necessarily from motives of biblical fundamentalism (though this element was sometimes present), but rather from an uncritical acceptance of the familiar outline of the biblical story, of which we cannot quite acquit Kenyon. But today's archaeologists have learned that biblical narratives must be treated critically.

Archaeology has also discovered other interests apart from the illustration of biblical political history. Archaeology's present concern is with understanding the settlement patterns in ancient times, the ancient use of land and methods of agriculture, food production, hydrology and ancient technologies, and with the structures of ancient societies – eco-facts as well as artefacts. Site excavation is accompanied by the detailed survey of the surrounding land so that the site can be seen in a wider context; and interest is no longer limited primarily to the biblical period but extended to all periods from palaeolithic times to the present. The number of regional studies is growing rapidly; one might note the Shechem area survey (E. F. Campbell 1968), work in the Negev (R. Cohen and W. G. Dever 1972, 1979), the central coastal plain (R. Gophna 1977), the Hesban region (R. Ibach 1976–8), Judaea, Samaria and the Golan (M. Kochavi 1967–8), Galilee and the Golan (E. Meyers 1978), and so on. Work of this nature – for example, I. Finkelstein's survey (1988) of Late Bronze–Iron Age sites in the hill country of Israel – has affected the interpretation of the biblical narratives of Israel's settlement in Canaan; it has completely undermined archaeological support for the idea of a conquest of the hill country from outside the land. On the other hand, it has been pointed out that Finkelstein's identification of these Late Bronze–Iron Age indigenous new settlements as 'Israelite' depends on an uncritical application of the biblical story to interpret his archaeological observations (as Horace said, you can expel nature with a fork but it always comes creeping back) (Bartlett 1989: 290–5; cf. Dever 1991a: 77–90). The surveys of Transjordan from Nelson Glueck's in the 1930s to those of Max Miller, Burton MacDonald and others in the 1970s and 1980s have greatly improved our picture, drawn hitherto mainly from biblical sources, of the history and culture of the Iron Age kingdoms of the Ammonites, Moabites and Edomites (see, for example, MacDonald 1988; Bartlett 1989; Miller 1991; Bienkowski 1992). The modern archaeologist has also learned to look for answers to questions about ancient populations and their political, economic, cultural and religious organisation and activities by beginning from observation of similar societies today, as well as by drawing inferences from observed patterns of ancient settlements. The dangers of reading back from the present are obvious, but nevertheless the questions raised are pertinent. The interests of classical historiography have been replaced by the concerns of anthropology and the social sciences. Someone has commented that the confidence now put in such social reconstruction is not unlike the confidence previously put in artefactual evidence by Albright and his colleagues. Not surprisingly, debates about method fill the journals.

THE VALUE OF ARCHAEOLOGY FOR BIBLICAL STUDIES

What value, then, has archaeology for biblical studies? Clearly, archaeology has thrown light on Israel's material culture – buildings, architecture, city planning, city defences, burial customs, religious cult, temples, synagogues, *mikva'oth*, water supplies, costume and jewellery, writing, trading, agriculture, domestic life, and so on. We can set Israel firmly in the wider context of the ancient near-eastern culture and understand Israel as part of the wider world. But few archaeological finds bear directly on the biblical narrative. The water pool at el-Jib discovered by J. B. Pritchard may be the pool by Gibeon of 2 Samuel 2:13. The Siloam tunnel in Jerusalem with its inscription perhaps speaks eloquently of Hezekiah's preparation for an Assyrian siege in 701 BCE – though a recent conference paper by P. R. Davies and J. Rogerson argued that the tunnel was built in the Maccabaean period. The tomb inscription of one Shebna in the village of Silwan across the Kedron valley from Jerusalem may be from the tomb of the man criticised by Isaiah (Is 22:6). The famous Moabite stone was erected in honour of king Mesha of Moab (cf. 2 Kgs 3), but while it witnesses to Mesha's existence it does not relate easily to 2 Kgs 3 (Dearman 1989). From Assyria we have pictorial records of such events as the payment of tribute by king Jehu in 841 BCE and the capture of Lachish by Sennacherib in 701 BCE (which the Bible does not actually mention), and from Babylon records relating to the imprisonment of king Jehoiachin of Judah and his sons. Such evidence does at least confirm that the Bible's historical records speak of real people and real events, even if they do not confirm the biblical reports in every detail.

Many, however, have tried to use archaeology to prove 'the truth of the Bible'. If Albright did not claim quite so much, he did use archaeological evidence to attempt to restore confidence in the essential historicity of the biblical tradition, and to discredit the scepticism of some biblical historians. The problems here are, first, that such attempts reveal a simplistic view of the nature of 'history' in the Bible, and, second, that archaeology, while it might provide evidence for the site of Solomon's temple, or evidence for popular cultic practices, has nothing to say about the validity of such ideas as the kingdom of God, or the meaning of the poem about the servant in Isaiah 53. The biblical student has to realise that the discovery of a ship on Mount Ararat or of the broken tablets of the law at the foot of Mount Sinai will not prove the existence of Yahweh or the validity of the interpretation put on the historical events (whatever they were) by the biblical authors. Archaeological research may once have found the tomb of Jesus and may yet find the grave of Moses, but such discoveries will not demonstrate the uniqueness of Yahweh or the resurrection of Jesus. And, thirdly, archaeological research has often offered more evidence, or less evidence, than was desired, at least in some quarters. The Bible, for example, totally ignores the existence of any female consort for Yahweh; yet recent evidence from Kuntillet 'Ajrud has suggested to many scholars that at least in one place a female consort of Yahweh was worshipped (Meshel 1992: 103–9; Dever 1984: 21–37; 1990b: 140–9). (Against this, however, see the paper by A. D. H. Mayes in the present volume.) The biblical picture of the patriarchal age does not give a modern historian's picture of the archaeologist's Early, Middle or Late Bronze Age (whichever one you take to be the 'patriarchal' age); archaeological evidence has not supported the biblical picture of the 'conquest' of the land, and it has suggested that the Omride dynasty in the ninth century had more wealth and power than David and Solomon a century earlier (see, for example, Dever 1992: 354–67). The picture given by the archaeologist is not necessarily the same picture as that given by the biblical historian; the two are interested in different things. Neither archaeology nor biblical criticism, in fact, can really be apologists for the biblical faith, though they may provide evidence of the material context in which we believe God acted or the incarnation took place. We may not equate truth with factuality, nor history with theology, though we may find physical remains of places where we believe or our ancestors believed God was present, and we preserve writings which contain our Hebrew or Christian ancestors' interpretation of the work of God.

A major debate has focused round the term 'biblical archaeology'. W. F. Albright approved the term, at least in a geographical sense, arguing that biblical archaeology covered all lands mentioned in the Bible. It was for him a wider term than 'Palestinian archaeology'; it was that archaeology which had any bearing on biblical studies (Albright 1969: 1). G. E. Wright, a pupil of Albright's, held a similar view; he identified biblical archaeology as 'a special "armchair" variety of general archaeology' and the biblical archaeologist as one who

> studies the discoveries of excavations in order to glean from them every fact that throws a direct, indirect, or even diffused light upon the Bible. He must be intelligently concerned with stratigraphy and typology, upon which the methodology of modern archaeology rests. . . . Yet his chief concern is not with methods or pots or weapons in themselves alone. His central and absorbing interest is the understanding and exposition of the scriptures.
>
> (Wright 1957, 1962: 17; see also Wright 1971: 70–6)

Professor Dever has objected strongly to the term 'biblical archaeology' because it suggests apologetic attempts to use archaeology to prove the Bible true. He has argued for the descriptive, regional designation 'Syro-Palestinian archaeology' (for example Dever 1985: 31–74; 1992: 354–67). This is not the same thing at all as 'biblical archaeology'. 'Biblical archaeology', he has argued, does not describe what he and his professional colleagues do. They are professional archaeologists who happen to exercise their professional archaeological skills in one part of the world rather than another. Archaeology exists as a discipline independently of the Bible, alongside other disciplines such as anthropology, philology, philosophy and so on. It provides an alternative perspective, which allows us to bring to light things with which the Bible does not concern itself – for example, folk religion, architecture, land use, etc. Archaeology has established itself as a separate, independent academic discipline, with its own scholarly agenda; it should no longer be regarded simply as the handmaid of historians or theologians. However, scholars such as Darrell Lance (1982: 97–101) and Alfred Glock (1986: 85–101) have argued vigorously that 'biblical archaeology' is still a legitimate term. Syro-Palestinian archaeology is concerned with Palestinian history; biblical archaeology is 'that subspecies of biblical studies which seeks to bring to bear on the interpretation of the Bible all the information gained through archaeological research and discovery' (Lance 1982: 100). It is concerned with the elucidation of the biblical text, and to be a biblical archaeologist is not to eschew scholarship. Dirt-archaeologists should not scorn the biblical scholar – though doubtless biblical scholars would do well to keep out of dirt-archaeologists' hair.

This leaves us with the question of how the apples and oranges of archaeology and biblical studies might relate. They are certainly two different, separate disciplines, and in fact two separate histories of ancient Israel, or ancient anywhere, can be written from the archaeological or literary, textual evidence. The artefacts need interpreting, the texts need interpreting. Artefacts and texts each have different origins, different contexts, and speak of different things. But both artefacts and texts are needed, even if they do not each necessarily throw direct light on the other. Axel Knauf argues that archaeology and texts do not meet, and wants to write a history of ancient Israel on the basis of objective archaeological evidence, which can be used as a context from which to interpret the literary texts (Knauf 1991: 26–64). But that is surely just as bad as using the texts as a context from which to interpret the archaeology. We must also remember that we put meaning on artefacts just as the biblical writers put meaning on events. The basic answer must be that the reconstruction of all aspects of biblical history is an interdisciplinary affair in which linguists, philologists, palaeographers, textual critics, literary historians, archaeologists and others all share. The archaeologist is no autonomous super-being; the archaeologist also needs the help of other specialists – architects, radio-carbon dating technologists, palaeobotanists, chemists, epigraphists, and so on. Archaeology is a discipline which, like all other academic disciplines, thrives only in the company of others; biblical archaeology, in so far as it exists, refers to that archaeology which has relevance to the field of biblical studies. One might speak similarly of industrial archaeology. In turn, the biblical scholar needs the expertise of the professional archaeologist to illuminate the biblical record. As Morton Smith observed in a famous presidential address to the Society for Biblical Literature in 1968, 'for a correct history of the Israelites we must have the archaeological facts determined quite objectively and independently by competent archaeologists, and the biblical texts likewise by competent philologians, and then we can begin to compare them' (Smith 1969: 34). I would qualify his word 'facts' to include interpretation, and I would not limit biblical scholars to philologians, but in principle Morton Smith was right. Misunderstandings occur when an archaeologist interprets an excavated biblical site by uncritical use of the bible, or when, conversely, a biblical scholar reconstructs history with the help of an equally uncritical use of archaeology. The history of biblical interpretation contains many examples of both errors; it is to be hoped that in future students of the text and students of the soil will develop mutual respect for each other's disciplines, and so will be able to co-operate in meaningful and productive dialogue.

BIBLIOGRAPHY

Albright, W. F. (1966) 'The Amarna letters from Palestine', in *The Cambridge Ancient History*, rev. edn vol. II, xx, Cambridge: Cambridge University Press, 3–23.

—— (1969) 'The impact of archaeology on biblical research – 1966', in D. N. Freedman and J. C. Greenfield (eds) *New Directions in Biblical Archaeology*, Garden City, NY: Doubleday, 1–14.

Alt, A. (1939) 'Edward Robinson on the identification of biblical sites', *JBL* 58, 365–72.

Auld, A. G. (1993) 'The British School of Archaeology in Jerusalem', in A. Biran and J. Aviram (eds) *Biblical Archaeology Today, 1990: Proceedings of the Second International Congress on Biblical Archaeology, Jerusalem, June–July 1990*, Jerusalem: Israel Exploration Society; The Israel Academy of Sciences and Humanities, 20–2.

Avi-Yonah. M. (1954) *The Madaba Mosaic Map*, Jerusalem: Israel Exploration Society.

Bartlett, J. R. (1989) review of I. Finkelstein, *The Archaeology of the Israelite Settlement*, in *Biblica* 70(2), 290–5.

—— *Edom and the Edomites* (1989), *JSOTSupp* 77, Sheffield: Sheffield Academic Press.

—— (1990) *The Bible: Faith and Evidence: A critical enquiry into the nature of biblical history*, London: British Museum Press.

Ben-Arieh, Y. (1979) *The Rediscovery of the Holy Land in the Nineteenth Century*, Jerusalem: The Magnes Press, The Hebrew University, and Israel Exploration Society.

Benoit, P. O. P. (1988) 'French archaeologists', in J. F. Drinkard Jr, G. L. Mattingly and J. M. Miller (eds) *Benchmarks in Time and Culture: An introduction to Palestinian archaeology dedicated to Joseph A. Callaway,* Atlanta: Scholars Press, 63–86.

Besant, W. (1886) *Twenty-one Years' Work in the Holy Land,* London: A. P. Watt for the Committee of the Palestine Exploration Fund.

Bienkowski, P. (ed.) (1992) *Early Edom and Moab: The beginning of the Iron Age in southern Jordan,* Sheffield: Sheffield Archaeological Monograph 3.

Braidwood, R. J. (1960) *Archaeologists and What They Do,* New York: F. Watts.

Brandfon, F. R. (1987) 'Kinship, culture and "longue durée"', *JSOT* 39, 30–8.

Bright, J. (1960) *A History of Israel,* London: SCM Press.

Bruce, F. F. (1967) 'Tell el-Amarna', in D. W. Thomas (ed.) *Archaeology and Old Testament Study,* Oxford: Clarendon Press.

Charlesworth, J. H. and Weaver, W. P. (eds) (1992) *What has Archaeology to do with Faith?,* Philadelphia: Trinity Press International.

Coote, R. B. (1990) *Early Israel: A new horizon,* Minneapolis: Fortress Press.

Daniel, G. (1967) *The Origins and Growth of Archaeology,* Harmondsworth: Penguin.

Davies, G. I. (1988) 'British archaeologists', in J. F. Drinkard Jr, G. L. Mattingly and J. M. Miller (eds) *Benchmarks in Time and Culture: An introduction to Palestinian archaeology dedicated to Joseph A. Callaway,* Atlanta: Scholars Press, 37–62.

Dearman, A. (ed.) (1989) *Studies in the Mesha Inscription and Moab,* Atlanta: Scholars Press.

Dever, W. G. (1978) 'Kathleen Kenyon (1906–1978): a tribute', *BASOR* 232, 3–4.

—— (1980) 'Archaeological method in Israel: a continuing revolution', *BA* 43, 41–8.

—— (1980) 'Biblical theology and biblical archaeology: an appreciation of George Ernest Wright', *HTR* 73, 1–15.

—— (1981) 'What archaeology can contribute to an understanding of the Bible', *BARev* 7(5), 40–1.

—— (1981) 'The impact of the "New Archaeology" on Syro-Palestinian archaeology', *BASOR* 242, 15–19.

—— (1981) 'Retrospects and prospects in biblical and Syro-Palestinian archaeology', *BA* 45, 103–7.

—— (1984) 'Asherah, consort of Yahweh? New evidence from Kuntillet 'Ajrud', *BASOR* 255, 21–37.

—— (1984) 'Yigael Yadin (1917–1984): In Memoriam', *BASOR* 256, 3–5.

—— (1985) 'Syro-Palestinian and biblical archaeology', in D. A. Knight and G. M. Tucker (eds) *The Hebrew Bible and its Modern Interpreters,* Philadelphia: Fortress Press, 31–74.

—— (1987) 'The contribution of archaeology to the study of Canaanite and Early Israelite religion', in P. D. Miller, P. D. Hanson and S. Dean McBride (eds) *Ancient Israelite Religion: Essays in Honor of Frank Moore Cross,* Philadelphia: Fortress Press, 209–47.

—— (1990a) 'Of myths and methods', *BASOR* 277–8, 121–30.

—— (1990b) *Recent Archaeological Studies and Biblical Research*, Seattle and London: University of Washington Press.

—— (1991a) 'Archaeological data on the Israelite settlement: a review of two recent works', *BASOR* 284, 77–90.

—— (1991b) 'Archaeology, material culture and the early monarchical period in Israel', in D. V. Edelman (ed.) *The Fabric of History: Text, artefact and Israel's past*, JSOTSupp 127, Sheffield: Sheffield Academic Press, 103–15.

—— (1991c) 'Women's popular religion, suppressed in the Bible, now revealed by archaeology', *BARev* 17(2), 64–5.

—— (1992) 'Archaeology, Syro-Palestinian and biblical', in D. N. Freedman (ed.) *ABD* I, New York: Doubleday, 354–67.

—— (1993) 'What remains of the house that Albright built?', *BA* 56, 23–35.

Doermann, R. W. (1987) 'Archaeology and biblical interpretation: Tell el-Hesi', in L. G. Perdue, L. E. Toombs and G. L. Johnson (eds) *Archaeology and Biblical Interpretation: Essays in memory of D. Genn Rose*, Atlanta: John Knox Press, 128–57.

Drower, M. S. (1985) *Flinders Petrie: A life in archaeology*, London: Gollancz.

Edelman, D. V. (1991) 'Doing history in Biblical Studies', in D. V. Edelman (ed.) *The Fabric of History*, JSOTSupp 127, Sheffield: Sheffield Academic Press, 13–25.

Finkelstein, I. (1988) *The Archaeology of the Israelite Settlement*, Jerusalem: Israel Exploration Society.

Glock, A. E. (1986) 'Biblical archaeology: an emerging discipline', in L. Geraty and L. G. Herr (eds) *The Archaeology of Jordan and Other Studies*, Berrien Springs, Michigan: Andrews University Press, 85–101.

Hayes, J. H. and Miller, J. M. (1977) *Israeli and Judaean History*, London: SCM Press.

Hodson, Y. (1993) 'The Palestine Exploration Fund: Recollections of the past', in A. Biran and J. Aviram (eds) *Biblical Archaeology Today, 1990: Proceedings of the Second International Congress on Biblical Archaeology, Jerusalem June–July 1990*, Jerusalem: Israel Exploration Society; The Israel Academy of Sciences and Humanities, 6–8.

Hunt, E. D. (1982) *Holy Land Pilgrimage in the Later Roman Empire AD 312–460*, Oxford: Clarendon Press.

James, T. G. H. (ed.) (1982) *Excavating in Egypt: The Egypt Exploration Society 1882–1982*, London: British Museum Publications.

Jenkins, C. (1930) 'Christian pilgrimages, A.D. 500–800', in A. P. Newton (ed.) *Travel and Travellers of the Middle Ages*, London: Kegan Paul; New York: A. A. Knopf.

Kenyon, K. M. (1939) 'Excavation methods in Palestine', *PEQ* 71, 29–40.

—— (1961) *Beginning in Archaeology*, 2nd edn, London: Benn.

—— (1951) 'Some notes on the history of Jericho in the second millennium B.C.', *PEQ* 83, 101–38.

—— (1957) *Digging up Jericho*, London: Benn.

—— (1974) *Digging up Jerusalem*, London: Benn.

King, P. J. (1983) 'Edward Robinson, biblical scholar', *BA* 46, 230–2.

—— (1988) 'American archaeologists', in J. F. Drinkard Jr, G. L. Mattingly and J. M. Miller (eds) *Benchmarks in Time and Culture: An introduction to Palestinian archaeology dedicated to Joseph A. Callaway*, Atlanta: Scholars Press, 14–35.

—— (1992) 'History of the American Schools of Oriental Research', in D. N. Freedman (ed.) *ABD* I, New York: Doubleday, 186–8.

—— (1993) 'The American Schools of Oriental Research', in A. Biran and J. Aviram (eds) *Biblical Archaeology Today, 1990: Proceedings of the Second International Congress on Biblical Archaeology, Jerusalem, June–July 1990*, Jerusalem: Israel Exploration Society; The Israel Academy of Sciences and Humanities, 13–16.

Knauf, E. A. (1991) 'From history to interpretation', in D. V. Edelman (ed.) *The Fabric of History*, *JSOTSupp* 127, Sheffield: Sheffield Academic Press, 26–64.

Lance, H. D. (1982) 'American biblical archaeology in perspective', *BA* 45(2), 97–101.

Macalister, R. A. S. (1925) *A Century of Excavation in Palestine*, London: Religious Tract Society.

MacDonald, B. (1988) *The Wadi el Hesa Archaeological Survey 1979–83, West Central Jordan*, Waterloo, Ontario: Wilfrid Laurier University Press.

Mazar, A. (1988) 'Israeli archaeologists', in J. F. Drinkard Jr, G. L. Mattingly and J. M. Miller (eds) *Benchmarks in Time and Culture: An introduction to Palestinian Archaeology dedicated to Joseph A. Callaway*, Atlanta: Scholars Press, 109–28.

Meshel, Z. (1992) 'Kuntillet 'Ajrud', in D. N. Freedman (ed.) *ABD* IV, New York: Doubleday, 103–9.

Miller, J. M. (1987) 'Old Testament history and archaeology', *BA* 50(1), 55–63.

—— (1987) 'In defense of writing a history of Israel', *JSOT* 39, 53–7.

—— (1991) 'Is it possible to write a history of Israel without relying on the Hebrew Bible?', in D. V. Edelman (ed.) *The Fabric of History*, *JSOTSupp* 127, Sheffield: Sheffield Academic Press, 93–102.

—— (1991) *Archaeological Survey of the Kerak Plateau*, Atlanta: Scholars Press.

—— (1992) 'Reflections on the study of Israelite history', in J. H. Charlesworth and W. P. Weaver (eds) *What has Archaeology to do with Faith?*, Philadelphia: Trinity Press International, 60–74.

Miller, J. M. and Hayes, J. H. (1986) *A History of Ancient Israel and Judah*, Philadelphia: Westminster Press.

Moorey, P. R. S. (1979) 'Kathleen Kenyon and Palestinian archaeology', *PEQ* 111, 3–10.

—— (1981) *Excavation in Palestine*, Cities of the Biblical World series, Guildford, Surrey: Lutterworth.

—— (1991) *A Century of Biblical Archaeology*, Cambridge: Lutterworth Press.

Na'aman, N. (1992) 'Amarna Letters', in D. N. Freedman (ed.) *ABD* I, New York: Doubleday, 174–81.

North, R. (1979) *A History of Biblical Map Making*, Beihefte zum Tübinger Atlas des Vorderen Orients, B.32., Wiesbaden: Reichert Verlag.

Peters, F. E. (1985) *Jerusalem: The Holy City in the eyes of chroniclers, visitors, pilgrims, and prophets from the days of Abraham to the beginnings of modern times*, Princeton: Princeton University Press.

Petrie, W. M. F. (1891) *Tell el Hesy (Lachish)*, London: Palestine Exploration Fund.

Prag, K. (1989) *Jerusalem* (Blue Guide), London: A. & C. Black; New York: W. W. Norton.

—— (1992) 'Kathleen Kenyon and *Archaeology in the Holy Land*', *PEQ* 124, 109–23.

Puech, E. (1993) 'The Ecole Biblique et Archéologique Française – The first hundred years', in A. Biran and J. Aviram (eds) *Biblical Archaeology Today, 1990: Proceedings of the Second International Congress on Biblical Archaeology, Jerusalem, June–July 1990*, Jerusalem: Israel Exploration Society; The Israel Academy of Sciences and Humanities.

Robinson, E. (1841) *Biblical Researches in Palestine, Mount Sinai and Arabia Petraea. A Journal of Travels in the Year 1838 by E. Robinson and E. Smith undertaken in Reference to Biblical Geography*, London: J. Murray.

Robinson, E. (1856) *Biblical Researches in Palestine and the Adjacent Regions: A Journal of Travels in the Years 1838 and 1852 by E. Robinson, E. Smith and others*, London: J. Murray.

Rose, D. G. 'The Bible and archaeology: the state of the art', in L. G. Perdue, L. E. Toombs and G. L. Johnson (1987) *Archaeology and Biblical Interpretation*, Atlanta: John Knox Press, 53–64.

Searight, S. (1979) *The British in the Middle East*, London and The Hague: East–West Publications.

Shanks, H. (1981) 'Should the term "Biblical archaeology" be abandoned?', *BARev* 7(3), 54–7.

—— (1987) 'Dever's "Sermon on the Mound" ', *BARev* 13(2), 54–7.

Silberman, N. A. (1982) *Digging for God and Country: Exploration, Archaeology and the Secret Struggle for the Holy Land, 1799– 1917*, New York: A. A. Knopf.

Smith, M. S. (1969) 'The present state of Old Testament studies', *JBL* 88, 19–35.

Stern, E. (1987) 'The Bible and Israeli archaeology', in L. G. Perdue, L. E. Toombs and G. L. Johnson (eds) *Archaeology and Biblical Interpretation*, Atlanta: John Knox Press, 31–4.

Strobel, A. (1993) 'Deutsches Evangelisches Institut für Altertumswissenschaft des Heiligen Landes', in A. Biran and J. Aviram (eds), *Biblical Archaeology Today,1990: Proceedings of the Second International Congress on Biblical Archaeology, Jerusalem, June–July 1990*, Jerusalem: Israel Exploration Society; The Israel Academy of Sciences and Humanities, 17–19.

Thompson, T. L. (1991) 'Text, context and referent in Israelite historiography', in D. V. Edelman (ed.) *The Fabric of History*, JSOTSupp 127, Sheffield: Sheffield Academic Press, 65–92.

Toombs, L. E. (1987) 'A perspective on the new archaeology', in L. G. Perdue, L. E. Toombs and G. L. Johnson (eds) *Archaeology and Biblical Interpretation*, Atlanta: John Knox Press, 41–52.

Ussishkin, D. (1982) 'Where is Israeli archaeology going?', *BA* 45(2), 93–5.

de Vaux, R. (1970) 'On right and wrong uses of archaeology', in J. A. Sanders (ed.) *Near Eastern Archaeology in the Twentieth Century: Essays in Honor of Nelson Glueck*, Garden City, New York: Doubleday, 64–80.

Watson, C. M. (1915) *Fifty Years' Work in the Holy Land*, London: Committee of the Palestine Exploration Fund.

Weippert, M. and Weippert, H. (1988) 'German archaeologists', in J. F. Drinkard Jr, G. L. Mattingly and J. J. Miller (eds) *Benchmarks in Time and Culture: An introduction to Palestinian archaeology dedicated to Joseph A.Callaway*, Atlanta: Scholars Press, 87–108.

Wheeler, M. (1956) *Archaeology from the Earth*, Harmondsworth: Penguin.

Wilken, R. L. (1992) *The Land called Holy: Palestine in Christian History and Thought*, New Haven and London: Yale University Press.

Wilkinson, J. (1971) *Egeria's Travels*, London: SPCK.

—— (1977) *Jerusalem Pilgrims before the Crusades*, Warminster: Aris and Phillips.

Willis, W. Waite (1992) 'Archaeology of Palestine and archaeology of faith', in J. H. Charlesworth and W. P. Weaver (eds) *What has Archaeology to do with Faith?*, Philadelphia: Trinity Press International, 75–106.

Wright, G. E. (1957, rev. edn 1962) *Biblical Archaeology*, Philadelphia: Westminster; London: Duckworth.

—— (1971) 'What archaeology can and cannot do', *BA* 34(3), 71–6.

2

ARCHAEOLOGY AND THE EMERGENCE OF EARLY ISRAEL

William G. Dever

INTRODUCTION

In theory, pinpointing the origins of ancient Israel ought to be straightforward: one could simply seek information from the Hebrew Bible (or Christian Old Testament), since this purports to be the true history of Israel from its beginnings. The people of Israel originated as a band of slaves who miraculously escaped from Egypt. They then wandered across the Sinai desert, where under Moses' leadership they met their god-to-be, Yahweh, and received his law. And finally, under Joshua, they conquered the land of Canaan, dispossessing its inhabitants and settling there themselves according to God's promise. In practice, however, the quest for Israel's origins is not that simple, because the Hebrew Bible is not really a 'history book' in the modern sense, and to its credit it never claims to be. The Bible is thus not 'history', but '*His*' story – the dramatic account of God's miraculous dealings with a particular people designated to become his chosen. The Bible is almost exclusively a sacred history, or 'salvation-history', written as it were from a divine perspective, since its authors claim to be inspired by God. Thus the Bible is scarcely interested in human, that is, historical explanations. It intends to tell us not so much how or when ancient Israel originated, but *why*.

THE NATURE OF THE BIBLICAL LITERATURE

To turn now from the Bible's overall motivation to the nature of the literature, we must remember that there are specific limitations in the attempt to glean genuinely historical information from its pages, for several reasons. First, the biblical texts in their present, highly edited form are all much later than the events they purport to describe. They date from the time of the exile or later, when Israel's and Judah's real history was over, and the remnant community was reflecting on its disastrous past, seeking to justify what had happened. Second, these highly schematised theological reflections were shaped by what we call the Priestly and Deuteronomistic schools of writers and editors. Thus the 'history' of Israel that is now contained in the books of Genesis through Kings is not un-biased. On the contrary, this 'history' is clearly the product of minority, orthodox, reformist, ultra-nationalist parties in later Judaism. The fact that the so-called historical books of the Hebrew Bible are really 'historicised myth' or 'mythologised history' (some would go to the extreme of saying simply 'fiction') has long been known to scholars. But the implications of this fact for writing history and doing theology have not always been fully appreciated in synagogue or church.

Given what we have seen of the limitations of the Bible as an adequate source for history-writing, it seems obvious that an external, less tendentious source of information would be desirable. And, beginning a century or so ago, that source for many has been archae-ology, which has brought to light a mass of factual data about the long-lost biblical world. This new archaeological information is incredibly varied, potentially almost unlimited in quantity, and has the advantage of being more 'objective' than texts, that is, more tangible, less deliberately edited. It is not too much to say, with the great orientalist W. F. Albright, that modern archaeology has 'revo-lutionised' our understanding of the Bible, particularly in helping to place it in its original context. But how has that revolution changed our views on the fundamental question of Israel's *origins* in history? And how may the study of texts *and* archaeological evidence such as artefacts combine to produce possibly a superior portrait of early Israel?

VARIOUS MODELS THAT ATTEMPT TO EXPLAIN EARLY ISRAEL

In the history of modern biblical and archaeological scholarship there have been several hypotheses, or 'models', that have tried to account for the data that we have on how Israel emerged in Canaan.

The conquest model

The oldest and most obvious model – long associated with such names as Albright, John Bright, G. E. Wright, and others – is that of military conquest. This model is drawn, of course, directly from the book of Joshua, which recounts how the twelve-tribe Israelite league invaded from Transjordan after spectacular victories there and at Jericho, then swept through western Palestine in a series of lightning campaigns that destroyed many of the Canaanite cities and annihilated much of the population. The twelve tribes then took possession of the whole land. There followed the period of the Judges, a time of cultural struggle and assimilation; and in due course the Israelite state arose, consolidating the earlier conquests and fulfilling the promise of the land.

This model has the merit of simplicity, and it adheres to at least one strand of the biblical tradition. But the model has fared so badly archaeologically that it has been almost entirely abandoned by biblical scholars in the last two decades, and it is overwhelmingly rejected by archaeologists. The full story of this model's demise cannot be told here, but the main points are as follows. One should bear in mind throughout this discussion that both the newer archaeological evidence on settlement-history and the famous 'Victory Stele' of Pharaoh Merneptah mentioning a 'people Israel' in Canaan *c.* 1207 BCE require a thirteenth-century date, rather than the fifteenth-century date found in older handbooks.

(1) The Exodus story is nowhere illuminated by references to 'Israelites' in Egyptian New Kingdom texts, or by the discovery of nomadic routes and encampments in the Sinai desert, despite intensive exploration of the latter by Israeli archaeologists. The one identifiable site excavated – Kadesh-barnea, where the Israelites would have sojourned for some forty years in the thirteenth century BCE – has no remains whatsoever before the tenth century BCE.

(2) Most of southern Transjordan is now well known archaeologically, but it is clear that the Edomites, Moabites and other sedentary peoples that the incoming Israelites are said to have encountered were not yet settled in the Late Bronze Age, indeed not until two or probably three centuries later. They were simply not there to be 'conquered'. As an example, the specific cities of Dibon and Heshbon, where great Israelite victories are described, have been located (Tell Dhibân and Tell Hesbân) and extensively excavated. But they were not founded before the twelfth–eleventh centuries

Figure 2.1 Map of some early major Israelite sites, with a few Canaanite and Transjordanian sites for reference.

BCE, and there are no remains there at all of the 'conquest' period (figure 2.1).

(3) The same is true of Jericho and 'Ai where great victories are hailed in the Bible. Both have been extensively excavated, but were abandoned much earlier (Jericho a thousand years earlier) and show no evidence of occupation at all in the thirteenth century BCE.

(4) One may list all the cities in western Palestine that are mentioned by the biblical writers as the site of Israelite destructions and then look closely at the archaeological evidence. In doing that it must be concluded that only *one* – Bethel in the hill-country near Jerusalem – has a destruction layer *c.* 1225–1175 BCE that could possibly be attributed to incoming Israelites, and even there we have no direct evidence for the cause of the destruction. Either the biblical

23

sites were not destroyed; not destroyed at the requisite time; or destroyed by other agents, such as the 'Sea Peoples' or Philistines.

In summary, the mounting archaeological evidence does not support a 'conquest' model of any sort to explain the cultural changes of the Late Bronze–Early Iron I horizon in central Palestine or the rise of Israel, and indeed renders such a model impossible.

The 'peaceful infiltration' model

Sensing the weaknesses of the conquest model, European scholars between the two wars (particularly Albrecht Alt and Martin Noth) developed the notion that the early Israelites had originally been pastoral nomads, some of them possibly from Transjordan, and ultimately perhaps Syria and/or Egypt. These peoples gradually settled in Canaan, largely without forcible intervention or armed conflict, toward the end of the Late Bronze Age. They may have been joined by other groups already in Canaan, such as the *habiru*, whom we know from the fourteenth-century BCE Amarna letters to have been a dissident group of urban dropouts and freebooters in the countryside, as well as other local elements of socio-economic and political unrest. Such fusion might have created a 'peaceful revolution'.

This model also resonates with the biblical traditions, in this case the stories of the patriarchs in Genesis and their apparently pastoral nomadic lifestyle. In addition, it avoids the awkward absence of archaeological evidence for Israelite destructions. There were none, since the process by which Israel emerged in Canaan was one of gradual, largely peaceful infiltration of urban Canaanite society by local pastoralists settling down.

Here recent archaeological discoveries have not been so universally negative, but neither have they offered any real confirmation, so this model has fallen into neglect or disrepute. That is partly because few archaeological traces of pastoral nomads in Late Bronze Palestine have actually been found (always a problem with non-sedentary folk). Thus we can say almost nothing about what the material culture of such pastoralist groups would have been like, or how it might compare with what we actually have in the slightly later Iron I villages that are now known (below). Furthermore, early scholars' notions of 'nomadism' and the process of the sedentarisation of pastoral nomads can now be shown, both from archaeological and ethnographic samples, to have been naïve or mistaken at several points.

In summary, it appears to many biblical scholars and archaeologists today that the notion of desert origins, or the 'desert ideal' of the Bible, is just that: a romanticised fiction of later writers about Israel's origins, projected back upon a past that was actually very different. Perhaps only a few of Israel's ancestors had ever been nomads.

The 'peasants' revolt' model

In the 1960–70s several American scholars of the socio-anthropological school, such as G. E. Mendenhall and Norman K. Gottwald, advanced a novel alternative theory. Derived from examples of modern peasants' revolts, or 'wars of liberation', this model saw early Israel arising from a revolutionary movement. This movement attempted to overthrow the Canaanite overlords and rejected the corruption of Late Bronze Age society, mostly in the fervour of a new religious vision, 'Yahwism'.

Here again, however, there is no direct archaeological evidence of such a 'revolt'. Furthermore, what disruption there is at some Late Bronze–Iron I sites is probably less the result of social unrest of any kind than the cause of it. (Social theorists often confuse cause and effect, which are indeed difficult to separate.) Finally, scholars in general have rejected the 'peasants' revolt' model on the one hand because it is too obviously a projection of modern Marxist notions of 'class-conflict' onto ancient Israel. On the other hand, it invokes as the 'engine' that drives social change an idealistic concept of 'Yahwism' that lacks any external corroboration and therefore needs explaining itself. No doubt ideological as well as techno-environmental factors *were* at work in the cultural upheaval that marked the beginning of the Iron Age in Palestine around 1200 BCE (see pp. 40–1). But the fact is that we know too little about Yahwistic belief and practice this early to posit something like that as the 'cause' of the emergence of Israel into the light of history.

'Indigenous' or 'symbiosis' models

One of the strengths of the two models we have just noted is that both view early Israel as stemming largely from the indigenous population of Canaan. Such internal explanations of cultural change are more realistic and prevent us from falling back on the kinds of 'invasion hypotheses' that are generally suspect these days. When one adds to theory the overwhelming archaeological evidence we shall now survey for the indigenous origins of most early Israelites, the case seems closed. The newer models, which are indeed bringing us to a near-consensus on 'indigenous origins', still lack a convenient label, but I suggest adopting Volkmar Fritz's term 'symbiosis'. This term stresses the common, local, overlapping roots of both Canaanite and Israelite society (and religion as well) in the thirteenth–eleventh centuries BCE, and it sees the process of change as relatively slow and complex, involving much assimilation. Only some such model does justice to the rich archaeological evidence that we now actually have for the Late Bronze–Iron I transition in Palestine (and for much of the rest of the southern Levant as well), and to that evidence we now turn.

RECENT ARCHAEOLOGICAL DATA THAT ILLUMINATE EARLY ISRAEL

For the past decade many archaeologists have been accumulating new data and slowly piecing together a radically different picture of Israel's origins and early development. The data come principally from two sources: first, regional surface surveys done throughout Israel and the West Bank by Israeli archaeologists; and second, the excavation in greater depth of a few key sites.

Surveys

Extensive surface survey, settlement archaeology and the use of demographic projections, and the investigation of site patterns and distribution, all in the context of ecological setting and subsistence, characterise a relatively recent and strongly interdisciplinary archaeology. That approach has made a major impact recently in Israel, and it is that approach that has forced us to see early Israel in a new light.

The principal surveys have been carried out in Upper Galilee by R. Frankel; in Lower Galilee by Z. Gal; in northern Samaria (Manasseh) by A. Zertal; in southern Samaria (Ephraim) by I. Finkelstein; in the Highlands of Judah by A. Ofer; along the Sharon-Coastal Plain by several scholars from Tel Aviv University; and in the Negev by various archaeologists from the Israel Antiquities Authority. Most of the basic data are unpublished, or published in preliminary form only in Hebrew, but an excellent and authoritative summary has

now appeared in Israel: Finkelstein's *Archaeology of the Israelite* / ✳
Settlement (1988).

The salient facts that emerge from these surveys are as follows.

(1) We have now mapped some 300 previously unknown early Iron I sites, most of them in the hill-country stretching from Lower Galilee to the northern Negev desert.

(2) Nearly all are small, unwalled hilltop villages in areas suitable for agriculture, with populations ranging from a few dozen to about 250–300.

(3) Very few of these village sites are established on the ruins of destroyed or abandoned Late Bronze Age cities in the central population areas of Canaan. Nearly all were founded *de novo* in the late thirteenth–early twelfth century BCE, in the hill-country or in the previously sparsely settled hinterlands.

(4) The village layout, with several clusters of nearly identical 'four-room' or courtyard houses, is lacking in elite structures (temples, palaces) or any kind of monumental architecture. The simplicity, homogeneity, and ideal adaptation of the houses to farm life seem to reflect an unstratified, kin-related agrarian society and economy, based on the extended, self-sufficient family as the basic unit of production and consumption (what economists call the 'domestic mode of production'). Lawrence Stager showed persuasively in 1985 that the configuration of these villages – the 'facts on the ground' – fits remarkably well with descriptions of Israelite life and times in the period of the Judges in the books of Joshua, Judges and Samuel. The individual dwelling, with living and storage accommodation for foodstuffs, several animals, and up to a dozen people would represent the *beit abh*, the Biblical 'house of the father', or patriarchal figure, the nuclear family to which every *geber*, or individual, belonged. The cluster of several houses, sharing common walls, courtyards and other features, would then be the biblical *mishpahah* or 'family', in reality a multi-generation extended family (the typical Middle Eastern 'stem family' today) (figure 2.2). At the larger level of organisation, the entire village, consisting of several such clusters, would be the biblical *shebet*, or 'clan, tribe'; and the entire complex of many villages would be the *benei-Israel*, or 'sons of Israel', that is, the ethnic group as a whole. These striking analogies between new and definitive archaeological data and a sophisticated socio-anthropological reading of the older, folkloric strata of the biblical texts suggests to me that at last we have brought to light the actual remains of 'earliest Israel'. If so, this is one of the most striking

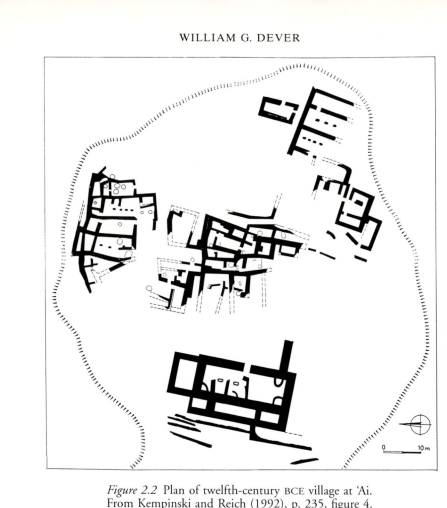

Figure 2.2 Plan of twelfth-century BCE village at 'Ai.
From Kempinski and Reich (1992), p. 235, figure 4.

success stories in the one-hundred-year history of biblical archaeology – the recovery of what I call 'proto-Israel' (more on this below, pp. 42–5).

(5) The pottery of these early Iron I highland villages – always one of our most sensitive media for perceiving culture continuity or change – is strongly in the older Late Bronze Age Canaanite tradition, exhibiting only the typical forms and the expected typological development. The highland village pottery differs, for instance, from that of thirteenth–twelfth-century Canaanite sites only in percentages of forms (more cooking pots and storejars) and in including a

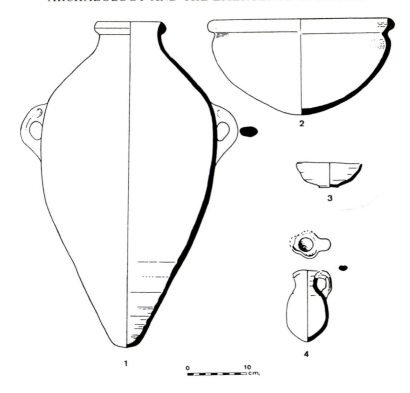

Figure 2.3 Typical twelfth-century BCE pottery from Giloh.
From Finkelstein and Na'aman (1994), p. 86, figure 8.

distinctive form like the well known large 'collar-rim storejar', which
we would expect more in rural than in urban sites (figure 2.3). This
pottery does differ somewhat from that of Philistine sites along the
coast, but principally in the lack of the distinctive Aegean-style
painted bichrome pottery – again, just what we would expect. The
most significant aspect of the pottery, however, which biblical scholars
have been slow to appreciate, is its *striking continuity* with the local,
Late Bronze Age ceramic repertoire. This pottery displays no 'foreign'
elements, no Egyptian reminiscences, and it is certainly not anything
that one could connect with a 'nomadic lifestyle' (we have such
distinctive pottery from later in the Iron Age, the 'Negebite ware').
This is standard, domestic Canaanite-style pottery, long at home
everywhere in western Palestine. The ceramic arguments *alone* would

clinch the question of indigenous origins for the settlers of the new highland villages; they came from elsewhere in *Canaan* (see p. 38).

(6) In contrast to the continuity in pottery, other material culture aspects of these villages are innovative and distinctive – what we might call archaeologically 'diagnostic traits' or even possibly 'ethnic markers' (below). These features would include the increasing frequency of rock-hewn plastered cisterns; underground stone-lined silos for grain storage; simple iron tools and implements; terraces for hillside farming; and, of course, the distinctive four-room or courtyard dwelling described above as the ubiquitous houseform (sometimes called, too simplistically, the 'Israelite house').

(7) Finally, there is no single feature that characterises the Iron I highland villages now known from surface surveys, but rather a combination of features, one that is constant and unique. I believe that this distinctive combination constitutes what we call an 'archaeological assemblage', usually typical of a socio-economic, cultural, or ethnic group – in this case, one that I would not hesitate to label 'proto-Israelite' (see p. 44).

Excavated sites

Supplementing the above surface surveys of sites, which are of course limited in information, there are several recent excavations in depth, whose results we can sketch briefly here, moving from north to south.

(1) 'Ai, north-east of Jerusalem, excavated by the late J. A. Callaway in the 1970s, has produced the typical layout of several courtyard houses, with Late Bronze–Iron I style pottery, a few metal implements, and a network of terraces on the nearby hillsides (see figure 2.2). There are several phases of domestic occupation, from the late thirteenth into the tenth century BCE. Noteworthy is the fact that, contrary to the biblical tradition, this 'proto-Israelite' village is not founded on the ruins of a destroyed Canaanite city. The *tell* had been completely abandoned since at least *c.* 2000 BCE (its name in Hebrew and Arabic means 'the ruin-heap', for it was a prominent landmark).

(2) Nearby Raddana, on the outskirts of the modern Jerusalem suburb of Ramallah, excavated by Callaway and Robert Cooley in the 1970s, is a tiny hilltop village of the same period (figure 2.4 and 2.5). Again it features clusters of crude four-room houses, shared courtyards, cisterns, typical local pottery, a few metals, and extensive nearby terraces. This small site, possibly biblical Beeroth ('wells'),

Figure 2.4 Pillared courtyard house at Raddana. Photo: W. G. Dever.

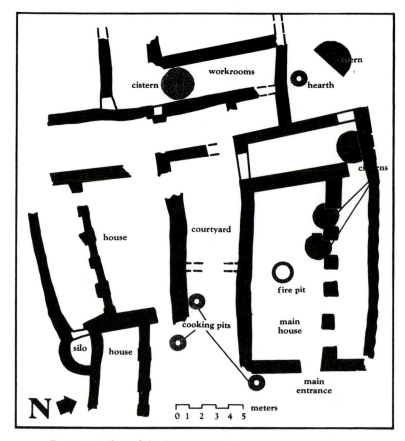

Figure 2.5 Plan of the house at Raddana shown in figure 2.4.
From *BAR* 9/5 (1983), 47.

represents the only occupation of the hilltop, extending from the late thirteenth century to about the tenth century BCE. It was, like many others, abandoned as early Israel slowly became urbanised during its progress toward statehood. One significant find at Raddana was a jar handle (figure 2.6) inscribed in proto-Canaanite letters *'Ahilud*, a name known from the Hebrew Bible (I Kgs 4:12).

(3) Giloh is another thirteenth–twelfth-century BCE hilltop village, on the southern outskirts of modern Jerusalem, excavated in 1978–9 by the Israeli archaeologist, Amihai Mazar. It is tiny, only a hamlet with a few early-style courtyard houses. Its ceramic repertoire,

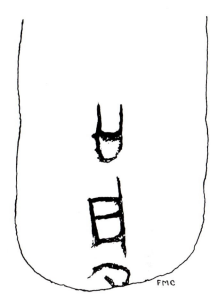

Figure 2.6 Inscribed thirteenth–twelfth-century BCE jar handle from Raddana, reading *'ḥl(d)* '(Belonging to) Ahilud'. From *BASOR* 201 (1971), figure 2.1.

expertly analysed by Mazar, consists mostly of typical collar-rim store-jars and flanged-rim cooking pots. It was abandoned as Jerusalem later grew into an urban centre (cf. figure 2.3).

(4) 'Izbet Ṣarṭah, located in the 'buffer-zone' in the low hills just east of Canaanite Aphek, may be identified with biblical Ebenezer, where the famous battle between the Canaanites and Israelites took place (I Sam 4:1, 2). It was almost completely excavated in 1976–8 by Israel Finkelstein in a modern, interdisciplinary project and is our most fully published 'proto-Israelite' site. Its occupational history is confined to the late thirteenth–tenth century BCE. Stratum III, the earliest, has only a few primitive houses, which Finkelstein has imaginatively reconstructed into a sort of oval plan (figure 2.7). He thinks this resembles a beduin tent-circle, which indicates to him a 'nomadic' origin for the settlers; but this view is contradicted by his own field supervisor, Zvi Lederman, in an article entitled 'Nomads they never were'. The pottery of Stratum III (figure 2.8) is typical of the earliest levels at the other 'proto-Israelite' sites we are discussing, although coming from an excavated site the repertoire is

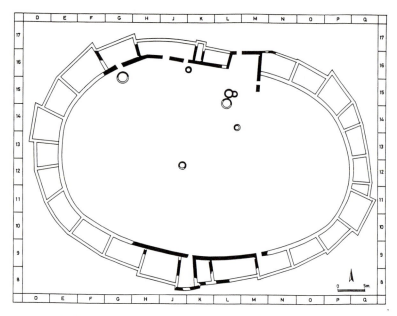

Figure 2.7 Plan of Stratum III, 'Izbet Ṣarṭah; only portions in black were actually excavated. From Finkelstein (1988) figure 76.

no doubt larger and more representative. Finkelstein has argued that this 'Israelite' pottery differs substantially from that of contemporary late thirteenth-century BCE Canaanite sites. But, in fact, the 'Izbet Ṣarṭah Stratum pottery is virtually *identical* to that of Stratum XIV at Late Bronze Age Gezer, a typical Canaanite site, only 10 miles away. Stratum II, of the twelfth–eleventh century BCE, exhibits several fully developed courtyard houses, surrounded by numerous stone-lined silos (figure 2.9). From one of these silos came a five-line ostracon, or inscribed potsherd, the bottom line a complete alphabet (or abecedary) written left to right in proto-Canaanite characters. Here we have another link between 'proto-Israelite' sites and Canaanite culture: script, and in all probability language (figure 2.10). (Scholars have long known that 'biblical Hebrew' is really a Canaanite dialect.) Stratum I belongs to an ephemeral eleventh–tenth-century BCE settlement, the last at the site. Of special importance is the exemplary analysis of the animal bones, seed samples, and storage facilities at 'Izbet Ṣarṭah. The result suggested to the specialists (if not to the archaeologists) that the 'Izbet Ṣarṭah settlers

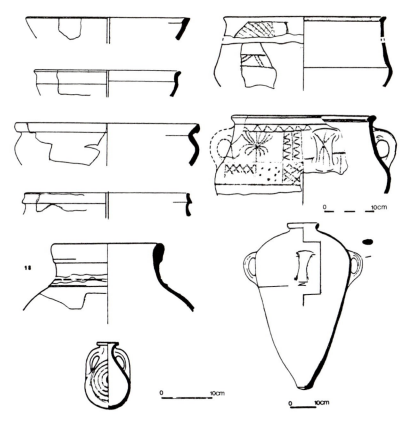

Figure 2.8 Pottery from Stratum III, 'Izbet Ṣarṭah, in the Late Bronze II/Early Iron I tradition, *c.* 1200 BCE. From Finkelstein (1988) figure 20.

were probably experienced and skilled subsistence farmers who were not only self-sufficient but produced a surplus.

(5) Tel Masos, in the northern Negev east of Beersheba, was excavated by a joint German–Israeli team in 1972–5. It may tentatively be identified with biblical Hormah. Again, the village has three strata, spanning the late thirteenth–tenth centuries BCE, a late nineteenth-dynasty Ramesside scarab dating its founding *c.* 1200 BCE (figure 2.11). The well-developed courtyard houses are built side by side, forming a kind of oval periphery (although not a true defensive wall). The pottery is somewhat more sophisticated than that at the other Iron I sites we have surveyed, including some painted Cypro-Phoenician

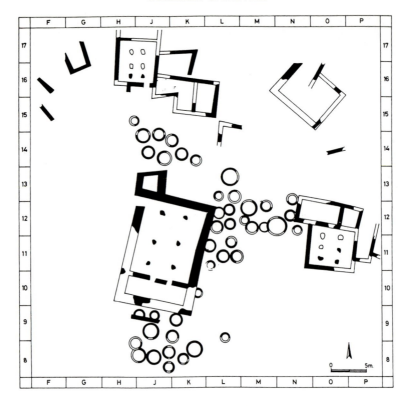

Figure 2.9 Portion of plan of Stratum II, 'Izbet Ṣarṭah, showing 'four-room' houses surrounded by silos. From Finkelstein (1988) figure 21.

coastal styles. That fact, plus the high percentage of cattle bones (*c.* 30 per cent), suggests to Finkelstein that Tel Masos is not an 'Israelite' site, i.e., a settlement of his pastoral nomads. But we should note that not even the biblical texts attempt to force all Israelite sites and groups into the same mould (see pp. 46–7). I suspect that Tel Masos is a 'proto-Israelite' site, but somewhat less isolated. Further-more, it was settled, like 'Izbet Ṣarṭah, not by pastoral nomads, but by experienced farmers and stockbreeders long familiar with the difficult agricultural conditions of Palestine, especially in marginal areas like the northern Negev.

(6) A few other early Iron I sites that could be considered 'proto-Israelite' have now been excavated, such as Mazar's 'Bull Site' in the

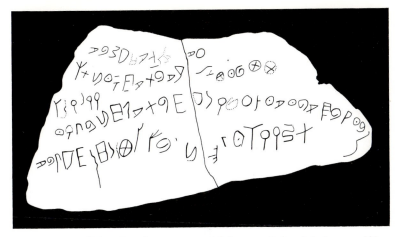

Figure 2.10 'Izbet Ṣarṭah ostracon, with letters of the alphabet, twelfth century BCE. From *BAR* 4/3 (1978), 22.

tribal area of Manasseh (figure 2.12). This is an isolated twelfth-century BCE cult site, whose bronze bull figurine is strongly reminiscent of 'Bull El', the chief male deity of the Canaanite pantheon in the Late Bronze Age. There is also A. Zertal's Mount Ebal installation of the same date, probably not cultic in nature. Another contemporary site, recently excavated and published by Finkelstein, is biblical Shiloh, near Bethel. Here, however, nothing of the early Israelite central sanctuary described in I Sam. 1 and following has been found, but only another typical Iron I hill-country village. It may be significant, however, that Israelite Shiloh is founded at a site that had some Late Bronze Age occupation and a prior Canaanite cultic tradition.

Clearly, many more of these supposed 'proto-Israelite' sites need to be excavated with modern stratigraphic and interdisciplinary methods, then properly and promptly published. Only in that way can we address the critical question of 'ethnic identity', that is, by comparing their material culture, economy and social structure (and possibly the ideology of their inhabitants) with contemporary sites that are presumably 'Canaanite' or 'Philistine' (see pp. 42–5).

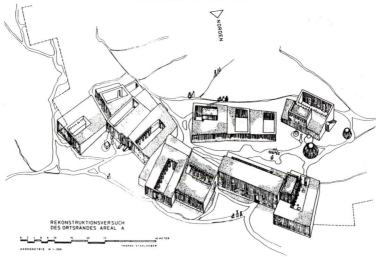

REKONSTRUKTIONSVERSUCH
DES ORTSRANDES AREAL A

Figure 2.11 Reconstructed early Israelite village at Tel Masos, twelfth century BCE. From Fritz and Kempinski (1983) 12, figure 2.

ISOLATING ISRAELITE ORIGINS
MORE SPECIFICALLY

If, as I have argued, the three hundred or so early Iron I highland villages that we now know represent the first settlements of the ancestors of later biblical Israel, can we say more precisely where their ancestors came from? That is, granted that these people seem formerly to have been indigenous Canaanites, not 'foreign invaders', *where* within Canaanite society and culture did they originate?

I have already given several reasons, both methodological and in terms of the most appropriate interpretation of the archaeological data, for rejecting theories of 'pastoral nomadic' origins. In the more extreme form of the theory, which Zertal holds, the early Israelites were nomads immigrating *en masse* from Transjordan. Here we are dealing with what I call 'secular fundamentalism', or reading the Bible in a way that is perhaps innocent of theological biases but still naïve. Amongst a few Israelis (not many), this may simply be dismissed as 'nostalgia for a biblical past that never was', or perhaps a thinly disguised archaeological justification for settlements founded by modern 'newcomers' here in the heartland of ancient Israel.

A recent, more serious full-scale presentation of the 'pastoral nomadic' origins theory has been offered by several of the Tel Aviv

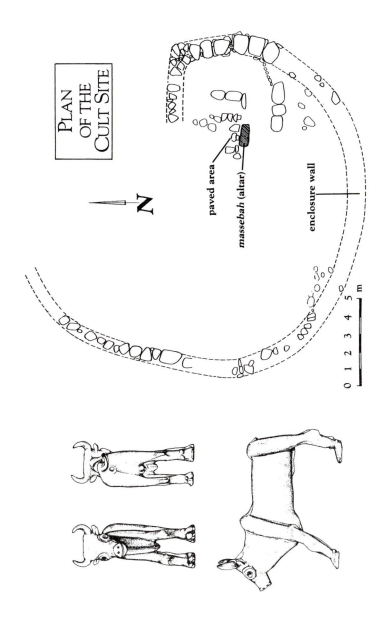

Figure 2.12 The 'Bull Site', twelfth century BCE. From *BAR* 9/5 (1983), 29, 40.

PLAN
OF THE
CULT SITE

N

paved area

massebah (altar)

enclosure wall

0 1 2 3 4 5
m

University scholars who have sponsored much of the recent survey and excavation, namely *From Nomadism to Monarchy: Archaeological and Historical Aspects of Early Israel*, edited by Finkelstein and Nadav Na'aman (1994) (figure 2.13). Even here, however, few if any *data* are presented that would corroborate such a theory, even in the attenuated form of local (not Transjordanian) Late Bronze Age nomads finally becoming sedentarised, as virtually all the essayists in this volume argue. I remain unconvinced and shall likely do so until we have more evidence.

Meanwhile, how can we most aptly characterise the lifestyle of the people we call 'newcomers', at least to the hill-country of Palestine in the thirteenth–twelfth century BCE? That is, all agree that there has been a major demographic shift by the twelfth century BCE. But what do these people *look* like when they first emerge as a separate group; how can they be recognised *archaeologically*; and what can that tell us about their immediate background? At the very least, some sort of 'label' for this group is needed, if only for convenience; and any label necessarily implies something about origins. We can hardly dub them simply 'the X-people', or, worse still, continue to speak impersonally of 'assemblages' or 'entities'.

I have argued, along with other scholars like Gottwald, that a proper interpretation of the biblical texts, extra-biblical literature such as the Late Bronze Age Amarna letters from Palestine and a few Egyptian texts, and the new archaeological data all conspire to suggest that the early Israelite community was a motley group. It probably consisted of some sympathetic Late Bronze Age *habiru* who became 'Israelites' for ideological reasons; many other dispossessed folk, refugees from the Canaanite city-states that we know were disintegrating, as well as impoverished peasant farmers from the countryside; and refugees, dropouts, entrepreneurs and adventurers of many sorts, all victims of the wholesale systemic collapse of Palestine at the end of the Bronze Age.

Among these groups there may also have been a few pastoral nomads settling or resettling now, as always happens in times of crisis. These may have included some of the *shasu*-beduin from southern Transjordan known from contemporary Egyptian texts, who seem to be connected with a Yahweh-cult there. There may even have been some escapees from Egypt who had been nomads in transit for some time and who eventually arrived in Palestine (below).

But in my judgement, *most* of those who came to call themselves 'Israelites' by the early Iron Age were in fact 'displaced Canaanites'

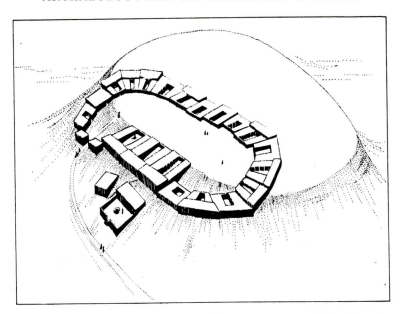

Figure 2.13 Isometric reconstruction of Stratum VII, Beersheba; eleventh century BCE. From Finkelstein and Na'aman (1994), 135, figure 7.

– displaced geographically, then culturally, and eventually ideologically. As Ezekiel has God say to his people Israel (not altogether as a compliment): 'Your origin and birth are of the land of the Canaanites; your father was an Amorite, and your mother a Hittite' (Ezek 16:2, 3). It was these people, still close to Canaanite language, customs and culture, who were the 'colonists' settling a new highland frontier around 1200 BCE. They were survivors of a period of cataclysmic upheaval and unprecedented chaos at the end of the Bronze Age, 'pioneers' in the true sense, seeking a new life and a new identity. Thus in the light of the newer evidence, early Israel may be best described as a newly emerged agrarian community, characterised by a close-knit social and economic structure, and probably also by radical, reformist ideology as has often been the case with such movements. (One thinks of the Shakers, or the Amish, or the New Harmony movements in early America.) Yet, as we shall see, ideology and religion (as well as 'ethnicity'), are much more difficult to specify archaeologically than material culture.

41

ON WHAT GROUNDS CAN WE SPEAK OF 'ISRAELITE' ETHNICITY?

Throughout this discussion of Israelite origins, it is obvious that we have been skirting the difficult issue of Israelite 'ethnicity'. Presumably the early Iron Age community that we have been describing, despite its Canaanite origins, came to think of itself in time as somehow distinct, as 'different', that is, as an *ethnic group*, a people (Greek *ethnos*). Indeed, I have argued that the material culture remains that archaeology has now brought to light clearly witness both the continuity and the new ethnic consciousness that we must presume. But what ethnic *label* shall we give the people of the Iron I highland villages? To put it more bluntly: what justification is there for the 'proto-Israelite' designation that I have been using all along?

Today many archaeologists and cultural historians are grappling with the complex problem of identifying 'ethnicity in the archaeological record'. Some believe that it is nearly impossible to do so, certainly without specific texts that supply the labels for us. Even so, such labels might be other peoples' terms, not the group's own name for themselves. And in any case perceptions of ethnicity (and that is what 'ethnicity' means, a sense of 'people-hood') are highly subjective and may change over time.

Thus the question arises whether we can legitimately apply *any* ethnic label to the archaeological assemblage and the population group that we are seeking to define here. After a somewhat optimistic beginning a few years ago, several scholars have just concluded reluctantly that we can neither recognise archaeological differences nor attach any ethnic label to them when comparing early Iron Age sites, especially in the hill-country. Several of the Israeli archaeologists in Finkelstein and Na'aman (1994) argue precisely that: we simply cannot distinguish between 'Canaanite', 'Philistine' and 'Israelite' sites. I am by no means that pessimistic. For one thing, real ethnic distinctions *did* exist, in the well documented multi-ethnic society of twelfth-century BCE Palestine. These diverse groups of people certainly knew who they were and how they differed; if we don't yet know, it's up to us to try to find out.

We have already made a beginning in isolating the hill-country complex that we have been describing here, which really is archaeologically distinct, even unique. We could go further, in my estimation, by devising a field project that would locate and excavate several small twelfth-century BCE sites simultaneously, with a single research design and strategy. These would be:

(1) a coastal site, presumably founded by 'Sea People' or 'Philistines';
(2) an inland site in the continuing Late Bronze Age tradition; and
(3) a hill-country site typical of those we have been considering as 'proto-Israelite'.

We actually have dug several such sites, but without the deliberate, systematic emphasis on recognising ethnic identity that would make direct and fruitful comparisons possible.

If we are able to recognise a distinct ethnic group in the archaeological remains in the Iron I hill-country villages, *which* group is it? It must be remembered that the so-called 'mute' artefacts are, in fact, supplemented by *many* ancient near-eastern texts (not only biblical texts) of the Late Bronze and Early Iron Age that document the presence of Egyptians, Hurrians, Canaanites, Philistines, Israelites and other actual ethno-cultural groups in Palestine at this very time. One priceless text is the 'Victory Stele' of Pharaoh Merneptah already mentioned, found by Petrie in the late nineteenth century at Thebes in Egypt, and securely dated to *c.* 1207 BCE. Among the various peoples over whom the Pharaoh claims a victory is Israel: 'Israel is laid waste; his seed is not.' The reading is crystal clear, and the Egyptian determinative sign preceding the word 'Israel' is that for 'people', not 'nation/state'. In other words, there was a 'people' some-where in the land of Canaan called 'Israel' just before 1200 BCE. And they were already well known to Egyptian intelligence, and already well enough established to be considered a threat to security in Egypt's declining Asiatic empire. If *these* 'Israelites' were not our hill-country people, then who and where *were* Merneptah's 'Israelites'? And how can we account for our hill-country complex if it is *not* 'Israelite'? Simple logic suggests connecting the two sets of facts (and they are facts); and if so, we have at hand the *textually* attested ethnic label that the minimalists demand. Better still, the decisive evidence comes not from the later and no doubt biased biblical texts regarding 'Israel' of the monarchy, but from neutral, external, contemporary sources. To put it in a nutshell, we have at least as much warrant for using the ethnic term 'Israelite' in the early twelfth century BCE for archaeological assemblages as we do for using the terms 'Egyptian', 'Canaanite' or 'Philistine'.

If the matter of affixing the label 'Israelite' is as straightforward as it seems, why do I hesitate and still use the term 'proto-Israelite', and in quotation marks at that? Part of the reason is simply that caution should always attend archaeological arguments in the early stages, before the data are sufficiently abundant to be definitive. But the most important reason is that the 'Israel' of the biblical texts really pertains more to the period of the united monarchy, beginning some two centuries later. When we reach the point of statehood – of urbanisation and centralisation – we can finally be sure that the population of central Palestine had attained a clear and self-evident sense of people-hood. All responsible scholars would argue that at this point we confront the *State* of Israel, whose citizens were certainly 'Israelites'.

The rationale, then, for employing the more tentative term '*proto-Israelite*' for the pre-monarchical period is precisely that here we are on the horizon where the later biblical Israel is in the process of formation, still nascent. But even with this precaution, how do we know that the 'Israel' of the Iron I period really *is* the precursor of the full-fledged later Israel, that is, of the Iron II period, so that we are justified in using the term 'proto-Israel' as early as the thirteenth–twelfth century BCE? The argument is really a simple one, and it rests on the demonstrable *continuity of material culture* throughout the entire Iron I–II period. If the basic material culture that defines a people exhibits a tradition of continuous, non-broken development, then it is reasonable to argue that the core population remains the same. Thus ethnic 'Israelites', preceded by ethnic 'proto-Israelites'. In time, with further evidence, I believe that we can abandon this tentative term and speak confidently of 'Early Israel' and 'Later Israel', with ample archaeological data to illuminate both.

Since continuity is so decisive culturally, it may be helpful to note here the specific archaeological features where it is evident.

(1) In the larger settlement pattern, the same areas that are settled in Early Iron I continue in Iron II and indeed form the heartland of the Israelite state, that is, Galilee, Samaria and Judah. That pattern is clear even though many of the smaller individual Iron I villages tend to be abandoned as urbanisation and centralisation increase.

(2) The innovative, distinctive four-room or courtyard house of the Iron I villages comes to be the standardised, indeed almost exclusive, house-type of Iron II, even in urban sites (thus the common label the 'Israelite'-type house).

(3) Burial customs, typified by the early Iron I borrowing of the bench-tomb (probably from the 'Sea Peoples', since it has Aegean

prototypes), continue into Iron II, where by the ninth–seventh centuries BCE the bench-tomb is ubiquitous at Israelite–Judaean sites.

(4) Pottery is perhaps the best indicator, with the Late Bronze ceramic tradition lasting into the eleventh century BCE, giving way to a traditional phase in the eleventh–tenth century BCE, then becoming a full-blown Iron Age Israelite tradition in the late tenth–sixth centuries BCE. In form, cooking pots, for instance, can be traced continuously right through the whole six centuries. In decoration, eleventh-century plain red slip changes into hand-burnished red slip, and by the ninth century BCE into wheel-burnished red slip.

(5) In language and script, proto-Canaanite develops directly out of Late Bronze–Iron I into a national Hebrew language and script by the early ninth century BCE at least, then continues little changed until the end of the monarchy.

IF THE BIBLICAL TRADITION OF ISRAEL'S ORIGINS IS NOT 'HISTORICAL', HOW DID IT ARISE, AND HOW CAN WE RESOLVE THE THEOLOGICAL DILEMMA?

Here we have to acknowledge another thorny problem, one that few archaeologists or biblical scholars have been willing to face head-on. To put it at its simplest, the picture of *indigenous* Israelite origins that the 'archaeological revolution' has virtually forced upon all of us is at radical variance with the biblical story of an exodus from Egypt and a conquest of Canaan. If we are right here, such events never happened, at least in the way the Bible claims. Furthermore, if there was no exodus and sojourn in the wilderness, there was no historical figure of Moses as the Bible describes him, the traditional giver of the law and founder of Israelite religion. Yahwism is then a later development, perhaps much later, not the cause of Israel's rise but the consequence.

The implications of these newer views, which have been so dramatically buttressed by archaeology in the past decade, are enormous, both for history and theology. The 'secular' explanation of Israel's origins as the result of a largely socio-economic and cultural change on the Late Bronze–Iron I horizon – simply another 'episode' in the long, complex settlement history of Palestine – would seem to undermine the very foundations of Judaism and even the Christian faith. If the formative events of Israel's early history

– the miraculous emancipation from bondage, the gift of the Law at Sinai, the deliverance of the promised land into the hands of the chosen people – didn't really *happen*, where does that leave us? Can faith and morality, or the life of the religious community, be predicated on myth? Few biblical scholars, and virtually no archaeologists, seem willing to confront these questions just yet.

First, it must be said forcefully that archaeology may have crystallised these problems, or posed them in a new way, but it did not create the current crises. Such questions were raised long ago, even within the biblical period. The problem of 'history and faith' has always been critical in religions like Judaism and Christianity that claim somehow to be historical.

Second, the 'secular' rather than 'salvation-history' approach taken here, and adopted necessarily by archaeologists who are not and cannot be theologians, does not necessarily rule out ideology, or religion specifically, as a factor in radical cultural change such as that accompanying the rise of early Israel. It is simply that ideas are often not recoverable archaeologically, at least directly. We may readily discover what ancient people made, how they behaved, and even something of the way their society was structured; but what they thought and believed is much less accessible. As the noted American archaeologist Louis Binford reminds us, 'Archaeologists are not well equipped to be palaeo-psychologists.' Archaeologists are even less well equipped to be palaeo-theologians. In the light of the built-in limitations of archaeology, we may allow some role for 'Yahwism' in Israel's origin, but we cannot say precisely what that Yahwism was, or how it operated culturally.

Third, there are in fact several ways out of the dilemma posed by substituting a modern explanation of Israel's emergence in Canaan for the biblical one. For one thing, we need to remember that the textual tradition of the Hebrew Bible as it has come down to us in its present form was shaped decisively and disproportionately by southern groups in Judah, as scholars have long known. Among these groups, centring around Jerusalem, were probably descendants of the old tribes of Ephraim and Manasseh, a coalition that the Bible sometimes refers to (or even all Israel; cf. Ezek 37:16) as 'the house of Joseph', the name Joseph being especially significant. Elements of this group may indeed have originally been slaves in Egypt and made their way to Canaan independently, perhaps making contact on the way with nomadic tribes in southern Transjordan who worshipped a Yahweh deity. That would account for the distinctive 'Joseph story' in the Bible, as well as the old tradition of Yahweh being connected with the Midianites in the desert (Moses learns of Yahweh through Jethro his father-in-law, a Midianite). If these newcomers to Canaan passed through Transjordan, entered Canaan via Jericho, and intruded forcefully into central Palestine, which was already a multi-ethnic society, that would help to explain some of the conquest narratives. Certainly early 'Israel' *did* include several diverse groups, with different origins, such as the Gibeonites and Shechemites, who according to the Bible 'became' Israelites through confederation.

We are presupposing, not without justification, a complex, multi-faceted process for the formation of the later literary tradition of the 'origin stories'. Thus we are dealing here with *literature*, which does not reflect 'real' life directly or even necessarily accurately – especially with ancient literature, which never claims to be histor-ical in the modern sense. Literature reflects life imaginatively. The biblical writers and editors are therefore interpreting events; seeing the past through 'the eyes of faith'; looking at monarchical Israel after her history is finished, trying to make sense of it all. When the authors of the Bible do look back, the fact that a small and obscure people from the fringes of the desert became, even briefly, a great nation; that despite their fickleness, Yahweh revealed himself to them through prophets and priests; and that even a remnant survived the Assyrian and Babylonian onslaught and kept their faith intact – all this seemed miraculous. It must have been God's doing all along. Such a conclusion may be somewhat skewed historically; it may seem naïve theologically; and it certainly cannot be confirmed archaeologically. But the Bible's 'explanation' of Israel may be in some ways as good as our own, for much about ancient Israel still remains a mystery, if not a miracle.

If we ask then how the story of the 'house of Joseph' became in time the story of 'all Israel', the answer may be deceptively simple. It was they who in the end *told* the story; and quite naturally, they included all those who later reckoned themselves part of biblical Israel. In time most people no doubt believed that they had been in Egypt.

A simple analogy may help us to understand this phenomenon. In mainstream American tradition, Thanksgiving is celebrated as though present-day Americans had themselves come to America on the *Mayflower*. That is the myth; yet in fact, most of the popula-tion arrived some other way. My ancestors came from County Donegal in the potato famine 150 years ago. Others came as slaves from Africa, or from the ghettos of Europe, or over the fence from Mexico. But spiritually (yes!), all Americans are pilgrims: that is what *makes* them 'Americans'. So, are the myths of Israel's origins, or America's, *true*? Of course they are – in the deepest sense. That we can put off our religious or cultural hat, and temporarily don the hat of the modern sceptical historian or archaeologist, does not necessarily alter or diminish the value of the tradition. We are what we believe we are, just as ancient Israel was.

CONCLUSION

In Jewish tradition, a vital part of Passover, which celebrates the deliverance from Egyptian bondage, is the recitation of the Passover *Haggadah*. The *Haggadah* is a partly historical, partly fanciful, partly humorous retelling of the Exodus story. In the prayers and blessings that are interspersed around the Passover table, in the *Haggadah*, which forms the libretto, Jews say: 'It is as though *we* had been in Egypt, as though God delivered us to this day.' I believe that the Biblical story of the Exodus and Conquest is best thought of as 'a Passover *Haggadah*'. Israel and Israel's descendants, Christians and Jews, look back at their own religious pilgrimage, this strange odyssey, and conclude that their own, unmistakable experience cannot be entirely explained rationally. They may be right.

BIBLIOGRAPHY

Ahlstrom, G. (1986) *Who were the Israelites?* Winona Lake, Ind.: Eisenbrauns.

Coote, R. B. (1990) *Early Israel: A New Horizon*, Minneapolis: Fortress Press.

Dever, W. G. (1990) *Recent Archaeological Discoveries and Biblical Research*, Seattle: University of Washington Press.

—— (1991a) 'Archaeological data on the Israelite settlement: a review of two recent works', *BASOR* 284: 77–90.

—— (1991b) 'Unresolved issues in the early history of Israel: toward a synthesis of archaeological and textual reconstructions'. in D. Jobling, P. L. Day and G. T. Sheppard (eds) *The Bible and the Politics of Exegesis*, Cleveland: Pilgrim Press, 195–208.

—— (1992) 'Israel, history of (archaeology and the Israelite "conquest")', in D. N. Freedman (ed.) *ABD* III: 545–98, Doubleday: New York.

—— (1993) 'Cultural continuity, ethnicity in the archaeological record, and the question of Israelite origins', *EI* 24: 22*–33*: S. Ahitvv and B. A. Levine (eds) *Eretz-Israel: Archaeological, Historical and Geographical Studies*, Abraham Malamat volume, vol. 24, Jerusalem: Israel Exploration Society.

—— (1996) 'Israelite origins and the "nomadic ideal": can archaeology separate fact from fiction?', in H. Silberman (ed.) *Mediterranean Peoples in Transition: Thirteenth to early tenth centuries B.C.E.*, New York: New York University.

Edelman, D. V. (ed.) (1991) *SJOT* 2 (entire issue has essays by several scholars).

Finkelstein, I. (1988) *The Archaeology of the Israelite Settlement*, Jerusalem: Israel Exploration Society.

Finkelstein, I. and Naʿaman, N. (eds) (1994) *From Nomadism to Monarchy: Archaeological and historical aspects of early Israel*, Jerusalem: Israel Exploration Society.

Freedman, D. N. and Graf, D. F. (eds) (1983) *Palestine in Transition: The emergence of ancient Israel*, Sheffield: Almond Press.

Fritz, V. (1987) 'Conquest or settlement? The Early Iron Age in Palestine', *BA* 50: 84–100.

Fritz, V. and Kempinsky, A. (1983) *Ergebnisse der Ausgrabungen auf der Hirbet El-Mšāš (Tēl Māsōs) 1972–1975*, 3 vols, Weisbaden: Harrassowilz.

Gnuse, R. (1991) 'Israelite settlement of Canaan: a peaceful internal process', *BThB* 21: 56–66; 109–17.

Gottwald, N. K. (1979) *The Tribes of Yahweh: A sociology of the religion of liberated Israel 1250–1025 B.C.E.*, Maryknoll: Orbis Books.

—— (1993) 'Recent studies of the social world of pre-monarchic Israel', *Currents in Research: Biblical Studies* I: 103–89.

Halpern, B. (1983) *The Emergence of Israel in Canaan*, Chico, Calif.: Scholars Press.

Hopkins, D. C. (1985) *The Highlands of Canaan: Agricultural life in the Early Iron Age*, Sheffield: Almond Press.

Kempinsky, A. and Reich, R. (1992) *The Architecture of Ancient Israel: From the Prehistoric to the Persian Periods*, Jerusalem: Israel Exploration Society.

Lederman, Z. (1990) 'Nomads they never were: a reevaluation of Izbet Sarta', *Abstracts, American Academy of Religion/Society of Biblical Literature*, Atlanta: Atlanta Scholars' Press.

Lemche, N. P. (1985) *Early Israel: Anthropological and historical studies on the Israelite society before the monarchy*, Leiden: E. J. Brill.

—— (1992) 'Israel, history of (premonarchic period)', in D. N. Freedman (ed.) *ABD* III, New York: Doubleday, 526–45.

London, G. (1989) 'A comparison of two contemporaneous life-styles of the late second millennium B.C.', *BASOR* 273: 37–55.

Mazar, A. (1984) 'The Israelite settlement in Canaan in the light of archaeological excavations', in J. Amitai (ed.), *Biblical Archaeology Today. Proceedings of the International Congress on Biblical Archaeology, Jerusalem, April 1984*. Jerusalem: Israel Exploration Society, pp. 61–71.

Neu, R. (1992) *Von der Anarchie zum Staat. Entwicklungsgeschichte Israels vom Nomadentum zur Monarchie im Spiegel der Ethnosoziologie*. Neukirchen-Vluyn: Neukirchener Verlag.

Shanks, H. (ed.) (1992) *The Rise of Ancient Israel*, Washington, DC: Biblical Archaeology Society.

Stager, L.E. (1985) 'The archaeology of the family in ancient Israel', *BASOR* 260: 1–35.

Weippert, M. and Weippert, H. (1991) 'Die Vorgeschichte Israels in neum Licht', *ThR* 56/4: 341–60.

Whitelam, K. (1994) 'The identity of early Israel: the realignment and transformation of Late Bronze–Iron I Palestine', *JSOT* 63: 57–87.

Zertal, A. (1991) 'Israel enters Canaan – Following the pottery train', *BAR* 17/5: 28–49, 75.

3

KUNTILLET 'AJRUD AND THE HISTORY OF ISRAELITE RELIGION

Andrew D. H. Mayes

THE PEOPLE OF YAHWEH

The Hebrew Bible presents a quite clear schematic outline of the history of Israelite religion. Israel took its origins in historical events and divine revelations which effectively defined her as the people of Yahweh. The foundation of the nation lay in her relationship with the one God, Yahweh. Other gods, indeed, there may have been, and into the worship of these gods Israel may from time to time have strayed; but this was, and was always judged to have been, apostasy. Israel's constitution at Sinai was as the covenant people of the one God, Yahweh.

In her subsequent history – in the conquest of the land, period of the judges, rise of the monarchy, monarchic period, destruction and exile – Israel followed a pattern of apostasy from and return to this one God. Not only did her settlement in the land present the temptation of Canaanite worship, but her adoption of the monarchic style of government and her expansion to become an imperial power exposed Israel to what was almost the necessity of recognising, if not indeed accommodating, the worship of other gods. She served other gods, but this was still apostasy, an aberration from the real course of her history and from her real character; Israel's true nature and history was that she was from the beginning the people of Yahweh. Theoretical monotheism may not have come to expression until the exile, but that was simply the theoretical and universalist elaboration of what had always been a practical reality for Israel: the acknowledgement of only Yahweh as God was essential to and characteristic of her true and original nature.

Israel was unique in the ancient world in this respect. The polytheistic context, in which the sensual experience of people in the

51

everyday context of agricultural life, in the political context of urban life, and in the military context of defensive and aggressive war found expression in the inter-relationships of numerous gods, and their interplay with the natural world offered an alternative possibility into which Israel as a nation and individual Israelites frequently strayed. But these acts of betrayal were just that, and were persistently classified as such in the harsh denunciations of prophets intent on bringing Israel back to the path to which she properly belonged.

THE HISTORY OF ISRAELITE RELIGION: A TRADITIONAL MODEL

This may be the traditional biblical view of Israelite religion. It can scarcely be called a history of Israelite religion, since for the Hebrew Bible practically everything essential was given at the beginning. Such changes as there were took the form of Israel's neglect of that given, rather than any progress or development in understanding or practice of that given. Nevertheless, such a traditional presentation is not without support both in terms of specific evidence and in terms of an overall scholarly model of understanding. As far as specific evidence is concerned, the impressive testimony of onomastic and epigraphic evidence cannot be ignored. The fact that Israelite personal names that appear in the Hebrew Bible are overwhelmingly Yahwistic might be put down to later editing, but the inscriptional evidence suggests a similar picture. So, it has been argued (Tigay 1987: 162f.), of the 738 Israelite names on inscriptions, 351 are clearly Yahwistic, a further 48 bear the theophoric element *'el*, which may be an epithet for Yahweh, while most of the remaining 339 make no reference to a deity. Only twenty-seven plausibly refer to deities other than Yahweh, and of these references it is only the reference to Baal in the names of the Samaria ostraca (five instances) which seem to fit with the constant biblical accusation that Israel went after the Baals. Yet even in this small number of instances, it is not clear that the Canaanite god Baal is the reference, for, as Hos 2:18 (MT) and 1 Chr 12:6 indicate, *baal*, with the meaning 'lord', was also a title that could be used of Yahweh. But even if all twenty-seven instances are references to deities other than Yahweh, the evidence still seems to suggest that Israel was an overwhelmingly Yahwistic society, to an extent that it would be justified to use the term 'monolatrous' of the religious practice of that society. The Hebrew Bible and the onomastic evidence could even be held to conform in suggesting a pattern of monolatry broken by apostasy to the worship of other gods.

Further support to this inscriptional and biblical evidence may be held to come from the theoretical arguments of Mendenhall and Gottwald, which have contributed to the development of a model of Israelite society and religion that harmonises well with the picture suggested by the inscriptions. Mendenhall (1962: 66–87) was the first to suggest that Israel's origins lay in a peasant revolt within Palestine, rather than invasion or infiltration from outside, and this was then adopted and considerably refined in Gottwald's ground-breaking study, *The Tribes of Yahweh* (1980). Despite the contempt with which Mendenhall rejected Gottwald's adoption of what he considered to be the obfuscation of nineteenth- and twentieth-century sociological language (Mendenhall 1983: 91), they both shared a view of Israel which is highly relevant to our present concerns: Israel's origins lay in a break with the past, a break with the context, and a totally new beginning. Mendenhall locates the primary impetus in this break in the religion of Israel, which creatively led to the emergence of the people of Israel; Gottwald, however, located the primary impetus in the social revolution which brought about an egalitarian society of which mono-Yahwism was the ideological expression.

Mendenhall wrote:

> A formative period is by definition one which is concerned to break with the contemporary and recent past, partly because it is intolerable or unsatisfactory, but more importantly because there comes about a vision and conviction that something much more excellent is not only possible but necessary. Discontent movements are a constant, as the history of revolt, war, and rebellion indicates. But rare indeed are those movements in history that result in such creative breaks with the past that they survive for centuries and expand over large population areas to create some sort of social unity or unified tradition that did not exist before. The first such movement to survive was the biblical one.
>
> (1973: 11)

> Religion furnished the foundation for a unity far beyond anything that had existed before, and the covenant appears to have been the only conceivable instrument through which the unity was brought about and expressed.
>
> (1973: 16)

> What happened at Sinai was the formation of a new unity
> where none had existed before ... a real elevation to a new
> and unfamiliar ground in the formation of a community took
> place – a formation based on common obligations rather than
> common interests – on ethic, rather than on covetousness.
>
> (1973: 21)

The terms of this understanding are thoroughly Weberian, and thus, despite Mendenhall's protestations, have an excellent sociological pedigree. So, for Weber, too, Israel's unity lies in a union of different groups in covenant with Yahweh. From a social and economic perspective, Israel was from the beginning much too diverse to constitute any sort of natural unit. The conflict of social and economic interests divided pastoralists from farmers and farmers from urban dwellers right from the beginnings of Israel. As the increasingly Yahwistic nature of the socially regulating laws in Exodus 20:23 to 23:33 and Deuteronomy indicates, what held these heterogeneous groups together was their common acknowledgement of Yahweh through the covenant relationship. The point of origin of this covenant faith lies in the work of the charismatic founder, Moses, and the laws of the Hebrew Bible represent the progressive rationalisations of that charismatic foundation for the establishment and development of Israel. The achievement of the charismatic, Moses, was a breakthrough to a basic insight from which new social and historical situations could be confronted, a breakthrough which came to be realised historically in the creation of the covenant community of Israel (Weber 1952; Mayes 1989: 41ff).

It is this rather idealistic reconstruction that Gottwald rejects as in the end ahistorical. The appeal to a charismatic founder is at the end of the day the adoption of an escape hatch which leaves the origins of Israel in unfathomable mystery (Gottwald 1980: 630). This is impossible for sociological method, and so Gottwald presses on to what he presents as a total sociological explanation of Israel and its religion.

> Israel's tribalism was an autonomous project which tried to roll
> back the zone of political centralization in Canaan, to claim
> territory and peoples for an egalitarian mode of agricultural
> and pastoral life. ... All the evidence for early Israel points to
> its tribalism as a self-constructed instrument of resistance and
> of decentralized self-rule. ... Israel's tribalism was politically
> conscious and deliberate social revolution.
>
> (1980: 325)

Early Israel's achievement consisted in this, that it brought together the diverse underclasses in the land which the feudal system had until then controlled and divided: the *habiru*, pastoralists and depressed peasantry. Israel's vehement and tenacious identity as a single people had its basis and focus not in a common commitment to the worship of one God, Yahweh, but in a common commitment to the overthrow of feudalism and the establishment of an anti-feudal, egalitarian society.

It is to this deliberately created egalitarian society of Israel that mono-Yahwism is, in Gottwald's view, dependably related. Mono-Yahwism, 'the innovative, non-philosophical, practical monotheism of early Israel' was 'the function of sociopolitical egalitarianism in pre-monarchic Israel' (1980: 611). This dependable relatedness means that

> the fundamental intention of Israel to limit the exercise of power by any one group...in order to ensure egalitarianism... enhanced the probability that the community would adopt or, as necessary, create a religion that did not usurp communal resources or communal power, but rather legitimated the egalitarian impulse.
>
> (1980: 617)

It was the social egalitarianism of early Israel that provided the initiating motive and the energy in bringing the Yahwistic innovation into being. Even though that religious innovation, once created, worked back upon society to preserve its egalitarian nature, the primary impulse lies with society, not with religious faith. Religion is fundamentally dependent upon society.

Now, it matters little to us at this point whether we follow Mendenhall or Gottwald. What is important is that each has created an attractive model of Israelite origins, history and religion that posits a sharp break with the past, a fundamental discontinuity in history, culture and religion, to the extent that Israelite society and Israelite faith are to be interpreted as social and religious innovations whatever their own inner relationship might be. With the adoption of the monarchy, particularly under David and Solomon, Israel experienced a return to the social and religious forms, indeed to what Mendenhall (1973: 16) calls the 'paganism' which, in her origins, she had rejected: a re-assimilation to Late Bronze Age religious ideas and structures with which, in her original nature, Israel was essentially discontinuous. But this confirms the general point: Israel

55

originated as a social and religious break with the past, and her essential nature is defined by that break. There may be some refinement necessary still in order to harmonise the inscriptional evidence with the sociological framework, in particular in relation to the degree to which Israel did undergo re-assimilation to the old pagan ideas and beliefs. (So, the Old Testament suggests the regular, comprehensive apostasy of all Israel, whereas the onomastic evidence would suggest that the worship of other gods was much more limited.) But both sources impressively combine to provide a model of understanding which essentially confirms the biblical picture: with Moses and the origins of Israel, history and religious thinking were fundamentally transformed.

THE HISTORY OF ISRAELITE RELIGION: AN ALTERNATIVE MODEL

The view that Mendenhall and Gottwald are in fact ultimately strengthening a thoroughly conservative and indeed almost super-naturalist understanding of Israelite social and religious origins is perhaps an unusual way of looking at scholars who are commonly taken to be representative of radically destructive criticism. Yet it does seem that this is the essence of their position. It is a position, moreover, which is in the end untenable, for the direct evidence, along with other more general theoretical considerations, leads to the necessary development of an alternative, more complex and much more credible model of Israelite origins and the history of Israelite religion.

The biblical texts

In the first instance, the use of biblical materials in the reconstruction of early Israelite history and religion has become much more difficult. The view that the materials of the Pentateuch and the Deuteronomistic History are simply literary creations of the exilic and post-exilic periods, and that it is to these late periods alone that they are addressed and of these late periods alone that they really speak, is probably an extreme reaction to an earlier unwarranted confidence that the traditions may be reliably traced back to the early periods of which they seem to speak.

Nevertheless, it must be admitted that the biblical texts in their present form are often centuries later than the events they describe,

that the concern of these biblical texts is not simply with the reconstruction of history for its own sake, and that the impetus towards
selection, arrangement and presentation of the Pentateuchal and
Deuteronomistic stories is rooted in the conditions and the issues
which dominated the exilic and post-exilic periods. The half-
millennium and more which separates that time from the origins and
early history of Israel is not to be glossed over and swept aside by a
superficial confidence in the powers of traditional literary criticism
to distinguish sources or in the ultimate reliability of Israel's oral
tradition. These materials are late, they project an idealised view of
things on to the past, and, moreover, they represent the narrow and
exclusive viewpoint of a very restricted, not to say elitist, group within
the Israelite community of the exilic and post-exilic periods.

Whatever about some of the detail, most certainly the model of
Israelite history and religion described at the beginning of this essay,
according to which everything essential derives from Moses and
Israelite origins, represents a back projection from a much later time.
There is only a distorted reflection here of the living reality of Israelite
religion through its history, a reflection refracted through the
distorting prism of the experiences of destruction and exile which
had created the need for new foundations for a new beginning.

Israel's covenant faith

This last point is the clue to a major aspect of our problem. Despite
the biblical presentation, despite the theoretical support provided by
Mendenhall and Gottwald, it is in principle problematic to speak of
'the religion of Israel'. (It is scarcely for this reason, however, that the
most recent and comprehensive Bible dictionary, the *Anchor Bible
Dictionary*, Doubleday, 1992, inexplicably contains no article on the
religion of Israel.) If 'religion' is understood in terms only of a particular set of beliefs to which people subscribe, then perhaps one can
speak of 'the religion of Israel'. But religion is as much practice as it
is the theoretical formulation of the meaning of that practice; religion
is the event that takes place as individual and community attempt to
relate themselves to the transcendent; religion is thought and action
bound up with the reality of people's particular concerns and experiences. It matters greatly, therefore, whether one is speaking of the individual, of the family, of the clan, of the tribe, or of the assembly of
Israel at the three major pilgrim festivals: the needs are different, the
concerns are different, the relationship established between the human

and the divine is in each case different. The rich variety here is not to be forced into the Procrustean bed of the covenant faith of Israel, or any other single schematic or doctrinal definition. To say that in all this variety there is, nevertheless, a common essence which may be defined as Israel's covenant faith, that covenant faith somehow forms the essential heart of the religion of Israel in all its manifestations, amounts to either a misrepresentation of the reality, or a vaporisation of covenant into a gaseous insubstantial category of no heuristic value whatsoever.

This point is easily demonstrated, and has, to some extent, been long recognised. So, it has been customary to speak of the theology of Mt Zion as the dwelling place of Yahweh, or Davidic theology as the belief in a special relationship between Yahweh and the Davidic king, and to locate these beliefs, and the religious practices associated with them, in the Jerusalem temple. It has been clearly recognised, however, that these are specifically Judaean, if not Jerusalemite, religious beliefs. Perhaps the precise social contexts of their relevance and significance have not always been closely noted, but their irrelevance to, particularly, the beliefs and practices of the northern state of Israel has always been clear. The to some extent novel development in more recent times, however, would seem to be this: that scholarly study is no longer content to remain at what may be called the political level, either in terms of history or religion, but is now much more concerned to penetrate to what may be called the social level. The political level is that of official practice, to do with the leadership, how it understands itself, justifies its role, and relates to the general populace and to other leaders. In religion the official level is that of practice in the temple in the capital city, the place where national festivals were celebrated, where the people, under the guidance of the leadership, are provided with the framework of national self-understanding within which they are persuaded to conduct their lives. This is the context where Yahweh's deliverance of Israel from Egypt, his gift of the land to Israel, his providing Israel with a chosen royal leader and a capital city, are all celebrated as saving events justifying and legitimating the *status quo* (cf., for example, Psalm 78). To be distinguished from this, however, is the social level, whether of individual, of family or of wider clan, where these are not the dominating concerns, where the lives of people are bound up with issues of much more immediate significance and relevance, issues to do with the birth of a child, to do with whether or not there will be a good harvest, to do with sickness and death.

It is the great merit of Rainer Albertz's work on the psalms in particular to have uncovered this level of belief and religious practice, and to have shown how the national saving history of the people Israel plays little or no part in family religion. So, in individual psalms of lament, such as Pss 22:5–6; 77; 143:5, the history of the people appears very rarely, and usually as an afterthought, while in the communal psalms of lament, such as Pss 74:2; 80; Is 51:9f.; 63f., there are frequent references to the historical saving acts of Yahweh.

> What is apparently so obvious a pattern of argument as 'You saved Israel from Egypt, so save me from my distress', etc., does not appear. Instead of this, the individual in his need refers to experiences of divine support and protection in his own life. His trusting relationship with God does not rest at all in the history of Israel but in his birth or his creation by God. That makes it clear why family piety can largely dispense with borrowing from Israel's specific historical experiences of liberation: the individual's relationship with God has its own, independent basis; it is deeply rooted in the creaturely sphere, in creation, and therefore is not at all connected with Israel's historical experiences of God.
>
> (Albertz 1994: 96)

Religious pluralism

The term which Albertz (1994: 95) uses to describe Israelite religion, at least for the pre-monarchic period, is 'internal religious pluralism'. This is useful enough, but it should not be taken to imply simply that Yahwism was the distinctive faith of Israel which happened to take different forms in different religious contexts. This is true, but it does not go far enough, particularly for the early period, for there is evidence enough that 'internal' should be taken not in the sense of 'internal to Yahwism' but rather 'internal to Israel'. That is, Israel's religious practice was characterised for a long period by its acknowledgement of not only Yahweh but also El, Baal and Anat, well known deities from the Canaanite context. The presence of Anat especially (Judges 3:31; 5:6) is confirmation that Baal and El are not to be taken generically as meaning 'lord' and 'god', with possible reference to Yahweh, but rather must be understood as the specific proper names of the Canaanite gods known by those names. The names of members of the family of Saul may be an indication of this plurality: his first son, Jonathan, has a Yahwistic name ('Yahweh has given'), but the second a name containing a reference to Baal (Eshbaal, 'man of Baal'). Jonathan's son, Meribaal, likewise reflects an attachment to non-Yahwistic religious practice.

It is only from a later editorial standpoint that a polemical anti-Canaanite attitude is introduced, in that Baal names, in particular, are given a distorted form. But the earliest evidence we have of an anti-Baal attitude derives not from the pre-monarchic or early monarchic periods of Israel's history, but rather from the period of Elijah and Elisha in the ninth century. For the earlier time, the worship of a plurality of gods was an accepted part of Israelite religious practice. To those gods mentioned we must add reference also to Asherah. There are particular difficulties attaching to biblical references to Asherah, to which we shall return in a moment, but it seems in the light of the plurality of the context of which we are speaking, and in the light also of what may well be divine titles of Asherah used in Genesis 49:25 (on the term 'breasts and womb', cf. Smith 1990: 16), that references to the Asherah and the wood of the Asherah should, for the pre-monarchic and early monarchic periods in any case (cf. especially Judges 6:25ff.; 1 Kings 18:19), be taken as references to the goddess Asherah well known from the Ugaritic texts.

Continuity and discontinuity

The picture which then emerges for early Israelite religion is thoroughly compatible with more recent understanding of the nature of Israelite origins, particularly from an archaeological perspective. The vast complexity of this topic cannot be even adequately alluded to here, but the general contours of what is perhaps the most probable understanding of Israelite origins are conveyed by this quotation: 'The Israelite settlement in Canaan was part of the larger transition from the Late Bronze to the Iron Age. It was a gradual, exceedingly complex process, involving social, economic, and political – as well as religious – change, with many regional variations' (Dever 1990: 79). More precision is provided by the following:

> Canaanite and Israelite culture cannot be distinguished by specific features in the judges period. . . . Items such as the four room house, collared-rim store jar and hewn cisterns, once thought to distinguish the Israelite culture of the highlands

from the Canaanite culture of the coast and valleys, are now attested on the coast, in the valleys and in Transjordan. . . . It is at present impossible to establish, on the basis of archaeological information, distinctions between Israelites and Canaanites in the Iron I period. The archaeological evidence does not provide a clear set of criteria for distinguishing an Israelite site from a Canaanite one, although a collocation of features (e.g. four-room houses, collared-rim store jars, hewn cisterns) in an Iron I site in the central highlands continues to be taken as a sign of an Israelite settlement.

(Smith 1990: 1f., 3)

The picture is in general clear: Israelite origins represent continuity as well as discontinuity with Canaanite culture and religion. The precise relative proportions of continuity and discontinuity may be difficult to establish, but the fact of a strong Canaanite heritage in Israelite origins and in Israelite religion is not open to denial.

KUNTILLET 'AJRUD

Kuntillet 'Ajrud has a particular contribution to make to this topic. The name, meaning 'solitary hill of the wells', is that of an eighth-century stopover station near springs on the trade route through the Sinai desert. It lies about 50 km south of Kadesh-barnea on the road to Eilat. Its particular interest for the present context lies in the painted scenes and Hebrew inscriptions which the site yielded. Inscriptions are found on pottery, stone vessels and on plaster. Storage jars were decorated with drawings depicting familiar fertility motifs and human or divine figures. Perhaps the most significant at this point is the inscription No. 1 and its closely associated pictorial scene. The inscription reads, in part, 'I bless you by Yahweh of Samaria and by his Asherah', while the painted scene, which partly overlaps the inscription, depicts two standing figures and a seated figure playing the lyre. The interpretations offered have been many and varied. Coogan, for example, confidently affirms a connection between inscription and drawing, holding that the two standing figures are the two deities mentioned in the inscription, Yahweh and Asherah. 'What Ajrud gives us is a rare, although undoubtedly narrow glimpse of both the texts and the iconography of actual Israelite cultic praxis' (Coogan 1987: 119). Others, however, believe that the two standing figures are representations of the Egyptian dwarf-god

61

Bes, who was widely represented in the Syro-Palestinian world as a god with apotropaic functions, while the seated figure is taken to be Asherah, described as the consort of Yahweh (Dever 1990: 140ff.). Yet others, taking the standing figures as representations of Bes, question that a major goddess like Asherah would be depicted effectively in the service of such a minor deity, and, noting that in any case Asherah is not otherwise associated with music, propose that the seated figure is simply a musician, though perhaps a royal figure, in the service of the god Bes (Hadley 1987: 188ff.). In any case, apart from the improbable interpretation of Coogan, it is notable that the connection between inscription and drawing has been effectively broken, so that it is as an independent work that the inscription should be interpreted.

On the face of it, the inscription is straightforward, but there are two notable features of it, at least one of which has proved particularly troublesome. One of these features is the reference to 'Yahweh of Samaria', a translation justified by the reference to 'Yahweh of Teman' found on another of the 'Ajrud inscriptions (thus, the possible translation 'Yahweh our keeper' is now generally understood to be highly unlikely). What these references indicate is a background and a context of a type of Israelite worship which is not directly apparent from the Hebrew Bible but which gives point and purpose to the deuteronomic proclamation: 'Hear, O Israel, Yahweh our God is one Yahweh' (Deut 6:4). The usual interpretation of this (cf. Mayes 1979: 176 for a discussion of possible interpretations), that it is an affirmation of the oneness of Yahweh by contrast with the multiplicity of the manifestations of Baal or El, is not wholly adequate. Rather, the deuteronomic proclamation is to be taken as a rejection of Israelite, Yahwistic religious practice, in which *Yahweh* was worshipped in different forms and manifestations within Israel. Yahweh, like Baal or El, was perceived and worshipped in different forms at different places, and the assertion of one particular manifestation rather than another carried with it political implications to do with the significance of the place with which he was associated. McCarter, on palaeographic grounds, has assigned the Kuntillet 'Ajrud texts to the beginning of the eighth century, and probably to the time of Jehoash of Israel (801–786 BCE). The political situation, as reflected in 2 Kings 14, was that in which Amaziah of Judah had been defeated by Jehoash of Israel who consequently held sway over Judah (McCarter 1987: 138f). The invocation of Yahweh of Samaria at Kuntillet 'Ajrud is at the same time an assertion of Israelite supremacy over this region of Judah. It is against this background that the deuteronomic assertion of the oneness of Yahweh must be appreciated, a unity which is at the same time an assertion of the unity of Israel.

The other feature of these texts, and one which is difficult to interpret, is the reference to 'his asherah'. That 'asherah' should here be simply the Canaanite goddess of that name, well known from Ugarit where she was the consort of El, and, as we have seen, well known also from the Hebrew Bible, is rendered very unlikely by the use of the possessive suffix, for such suffixes are not otherwise found used with proper names. The fact that proper names do, however, appear in the construct state (as, for example, Yahweh of Samaria, Bethlehem of Judah, Ur of the Chaldees; cf. also Dahood 1970: 262f., for the possibility that Ps 135:21 should be read as 'Yahweh of Zion' rather than 'Yahweh from Zion'), certainly indicates that their usage is not confined to the absolute state, and so the possibility of the attachment of a suffix is not to be ruled out. Yet, the general evidence is against 'asherah' in these texts being taken as a proper name (Smith 1990: 86).

It is certainly the case that Asherah was a goddess worshipped in Palestine. There are references to her as consort of El in the Ugaritic texts, and, occasionally, in the Hebrew Bible, as a goddess for whom or of whom an image was made and who had her own prophets (1 Kgs 15:13; 18:19; 2 Kgs 21:17; 23:4, 7). On the other hand, however, the majority of usages of the term '*asherah*' in the Hebrew Bible are with reference to an object in the sanctuary, a wooden object or pole which had a cultic function (Ex 34:13; Deut 7:5; 1 Kgs 14:15, 23; 16:33; 2 Kgs 13:16; 17:10; 18:14; 21:3; 23:14). With this, one should connect the fact that the tree was the Canaanite symbol of the goddess, and the stylised tree on the reverse of one of the inscribed pieces of pottery at Kuntillet 'Ajrud is very likely such a symbol (Smith 1990: 82; Hadley 1987: 196ff.). The *asherah* was, therefore, not simply the proper name of the goddess, but also a common noun denoting the wooden symbol of the goddess set up in the cult. It is to this symbol that reference is probably made in the Kuntillet 'Ajrud inscriptions: the asherah is the cult symbol which is set up in the Israelite sanctuary as a cult object in the Yahwistic cult.

One must note, however, that the reference is to '*his* asherah'. The force of that possessive suffix has not yet been adequately brought out: why 'his asherah' rather than simply 'the asherah', especially if the asherah was a wooden symbol of the goddess? It is here that one must return to the larger question of the comprehensive model of Israelite religious history into which the inscriptional material is to be fitted.

CONCLUSION

If the model described at the beginning is inadequate, and that must surely be the case, the development of an alternative must be undertaken. This alternative will have to take account of at least two established points. On the one hand, at the beginning of its history Israel's religious practice was pluralistic, including the acknowledgement of a number of gods; secondly, in the post-exilic period, her religious practice was monolatrous and her theology monotheistic. The history of Israelite religion is the course of development of her religious history that relates these two points.

There are two stages in this course of development which can be plotted fairly certainly, and within this general context the use of the term 'his asherah' may be fitted. The two stages are reflected in the formula: Yahweh is the God of Israel; Israel is the people of Yahweh. This formula expresses not just one idea but two, and these two stand in chronological succession. On the one hand, Yahweh is the God of Israel, and, on the other, Israel is the people of Yahweh (Mayes 1993: 26ff.). Yahweh became the God of Israel in the sense that it was only of Israel that Yahweh was God, before Israel became the people of Yahweh in the sense that Israel acknowledged only Yahweh. The historical processes involved in Yahweh's becoming the God of Israel can no longer be reconstructed in detail, but they go back to Israel's early period and are by no means incompatible with Israelite acknowledgement of other gods. Yahweh was the god of Israel in the sense that Chemosh was the god of Moab and Ashur of Assyria. In many respects the more decisive step is the second one, for it is now that this relationship between Yahweh and Israel becomes exclusive and Israel is the people of Yahweh alone. Such a Yahweh-alone development can be traced in Israel to the activity of the prophets Elijah and Elisha in the ninth century. This was a politico-religious movement very much bound up with the assertion of cultural values *within* Israel, and not simply with an anti-Canaanite movement on the part of Israel as a whole. The adoption of the programme of the movement by the classical prophets of the northern kingdom, and the subsequent destruction of the northern kingdom by the Assyrians created a fateful link between political crisis and neglect of Yahweh. The succession of crises which marked the remaining years of the southern kingdom ensured the increasing strength and influence of that movement, coming to expression in the reforms of Hezekiah and Josiah, and culminating in the deuteronomic demand for Israel's exclusive attachment to Yahweh alone at a single sanctuary.

A major and exceedingly significant feature of this whole history was a two-sided process of identification and rejection, of convergence and differentiation (Smith 1990: 21ff.). Yahweh was over the course of time identified with other gods, particularly El, and characteristic features of the understanding of El, to do especially with creation and kingship, were absorbed into the Israelite understanding of Yahweh. It was undoubtedly this process of convergence, of the absorption by Yahweh of other gods, which facilitated the gradual development towards the exclusiveness of Yahweh. Now, it is not unlikely that the phrase 'his asherah', Yahweh's asherah, should be understood in this way: just as with El and his kingship, so also with Asherah and her rituals, the worship of Yahweh was enriched by the syncretistic adoption of language and practices which had originally been related to the worship of another deity. Attention has been drawn to the fertility imagery which informs descriptions of Yahweh in some prophetic texts, such as Hos 14:9 (cf. particularly Wellhausen's proposed emendation of this text to read 'I am his Anat and his Asherah', noted in Wolff 1974: 233). In addition, the prophetic and deuteronomic polemic against what is identified as cultic prostitution (Hos 4:11–14; Deut 23:18f.) is not necessarily to be taken as rejection of Canaanite fertility religion but rather as a rejection of what had come to be an accepted feature of the Israelite worship of Yahweh in this syncretistic period of convergence. Yahweh's asherah is to be related to the absorption of the theology and practice of the worship of Asherah into Yahwistic religion. In deuteronomic polemic, however, Yahweh's asherah is reduced simply to 'the asherah', a cult object which must be destroyed, and is sharply differentiated from what has come to be seen as the only acceptable form of acknowledgement of Yahweh, a form established essentially by prophetic preaching. Kuntillet 'Ajrud offers a glimpse of a stage of Israelite religious history in which a rich, even if potentially dangerous, expression of the theology and practice of the worship of Yahweh was prevalent in Israel.

BIBLIOGRAPHY

Albertz, R. (1994) *A History of Israelite Religion*, London: SCM Press.

Coogan, M. D. (1987) 'Canaanite origins and lineage: reflections on the religion of ancient Israel', in P. D. Miller, P. D. Hanson and S. Dean McBride (eds) *Ancient Israelite Religion: Essays in Honor of Frank Moore Cross*, Philadelphia: Fortress Press, 115–24.

Dahood, M. J. (1970) *Psalms I–III* (Anchor Bible Commentary), Garden City, New York: Doubleday.

Dever, W. G. (1990) *Recent Archaeological Discoveries and Biblical Research*, Seattle and London: University of Washington Press.

Gottwald, N. (1980) *The Tribes of Yahweh: A sociology of the religion of liberated Israel, 1250–1050 B.C.E.*, London: SCM Press.

Hadley, J. M. (1987) 'Some drawings and inscriptions on two pithoi from Kuntillet Ajrud', *VT* 37, 180–213.

McCarter, P. Kyle (1987) 'Aspects of the religion of the Israelite monarchy: biblical and epigraphic data', in P. D. Miller, P. D. Hanson and S. Dean McBride (eds) *Ancient Israelite Religion: Essays in honor of Frank Moore Cross*, Philadelphia: Fortress Press, 137–55.

Mayes, A. D. H. (1979) *Deuteronomy* (New Century Bible), London: Oliphants.

—— (1989) *The Old Testament in Sociological Perspective*, London: Marshall and Pickering.

—— (1993) 'The emergence of monotheism in Israel', in J. M. Byrne (ed.) *The Christian Understanding of God Today*, Dublin: Columba Press, 26–33.

Mendenhall, G. E. (1962) 'The Hebrew conquest of Palestine', *BA* 25, 66–87.

—— (1973) *The Tenth Generation: The origins of the biblical tradition*, Baltimore: Johns Hopkins University Press.

—— (1983) 'Ancient Israel's hyphenated history', in D. N. Freedman and D. F. Graf (eds) *Palestine in Transition: The emergence of ancient Israel*, Sheffield: Sheffield University Press.

Smith, M. S. (1990) *The Early History of God: Yahweh and the other deities in ancient Israel*, New York: Harper and Row.

Tigay, J. H. (1987) 'Israelite religion: the onomastic and epigraphic evidence', in P. D. Miller, P. D. Hanson and S. D. McBride (eds) *Ancient Israelite Religion: Essays in honor of Frank Moore Cross*, Philadelphia: Fortress Press, 157–94.

Weber, M. (1952) *Ancient Judaism*, trans. and ed. by H. H. Gerth and D. Martindale, New York: The Free Press; London: Collier-Macmillan.

Wolff, H. W. (1974) *Hosea* (Hermeneia), Philadelphia: Fortress Press.

4

THE ARCHAEOLOGY OF QUMRAN

John R. Bartlett

KHIRBET QUMRAN

Khirbet Qumran, the ruin of Qumran, is a small site built on a marl terrace at the foot of the limestone cliffs at the northwest end of the Dead Sea. The cliffs (over 300 m high) are part of the west side of the great rift valley which stretches from Syria to east central Africa; the grey Lisan marl between the cliffs and the Dead Sea is the deposit left by the huge Lisan lake which once filled the Palestinian section of the rift valley; and the Dead Sea is the remaining fragment of that once much larger and deeper lake. The limestone cliffs are a difficult area, full of deep clefts and small caves; the marl is barren wasteland; and the two areas support little but goats; but agriculture is practised round the better springs and especially round the oasis of Jericho, several miles to the north.

Khirbet Qumran was known to and described by several travellers of the nineteenth century. In 1851, Ferdinand de Saulcy travelled south down the west coast of the Dead Sea past Wadi Qumran, where he noticed a square cave 'at an elevation of a hundred yards above our road', down to 'Ain Feshka and Khirbet el-Yahud, and then back again'. His account is very confusing, because at one point he locates Kh. el-Yahoud (as he names it) north of 'Ain Feshka while his map puts it south (see figure 4.1); but north of Kh. el-Yahud he lists in sequence a hill covered with ruins, the skeleton of a large city still called by the Arabs Khirbet Feshkah, a long wall and square enclosure, the opening of wadi Qumran fronted by two mounds of compact sand and a very apparent square ruin particularly called the Khirbet Feshkah, and then 'from the head of the Ouad Goumran, the extensive ruins which we have found on our way bear the name of Kharbet Goumran or Oumran' (which de Saulcy identified with

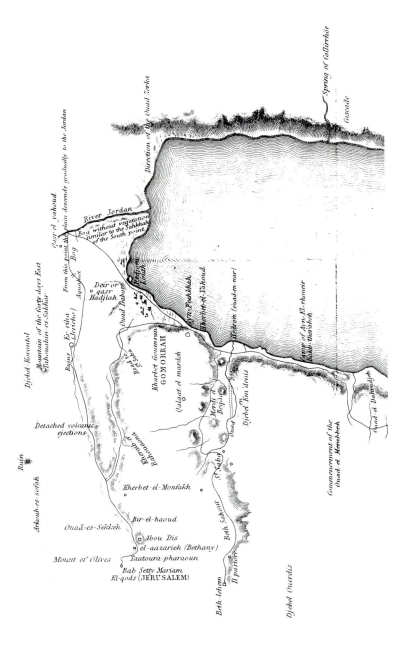

Figure 4.1 F. de Saulcy's map of the Qumran area. From F. de Saulcy (1853).

Spring of Callirrhoë

Cascade

Direction of the Ouad Zerka

River Jordan

Qasr el rahoud

Bog without vegetation similar to the Sahkhah of the South Point

From this point the plain descends gradually to the Jordan

Mountain of the forty days Fast
Tahoulan-es-Sakhar

Djebel Korontol

Aqueduct

Deir or qasr Hadjlah

Bog

Ruins El-rihn (Jericho)

Medbon Houdah

Ouad Dabon

Eyn Feshkhah

Kherbet-el-Tahoud

Widron (ouad-en-nar)

Cantle of Ayn-El-ghouer
Widai theïrûbeh

Kharbet Goumran
GOMORRAH

Qalaat el marith

Merid el Bcijlah

Djebel Em deus

Commencement of the Ouad el Membkeh

Ouad el Dabousjeh

Detached volcanic ejections

Bogd Saun

Ouad el Sebaa

Ouad Roubrand

St Saba

Beth Sahour

Ruin

Arkoub-es-sofah

Kherbet-el-Monfakh

Bir-el-haoud

Ouad-es-Sekkeh

Abou Dis

el-aazarieh (Bethany)

Tautoura-pharaoun

Mount or Olives

Bab Setty Mariam
El-qods (JERUSALEM)

Beth-lehem

Il pastori

Djebel Ouardis

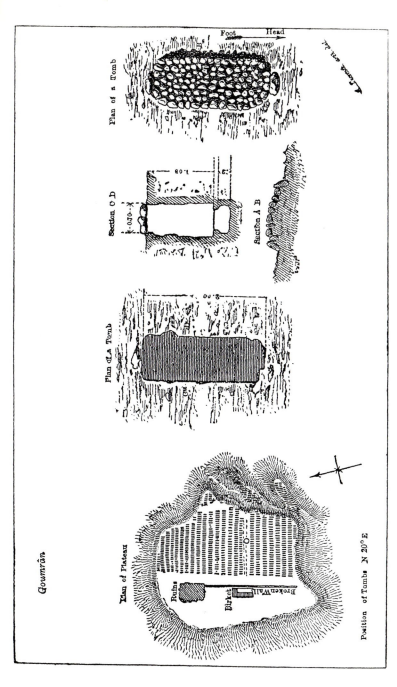

Figure 4.2 Clermont-Ganneau's illustration of the 'Cemetery of Goumran'. From *PEFQS* (1874), 81.

biblical Gomorrah) (de Saulcy 1853: II. 54–63). In 1873 Clermont-
Ganneau visited Qumran and noted the ruins: 'quite insignificant
in themselves: a few fallen walls of mean construction; a little birket,
into which you descend by steps; and numerous fragments of irreg-
ular pottery. . .' – and numerous tombs, distinguished by their
north–south orientation from the Muslim tombs. He drew a rough
plan of 'this enigmatical cemetery' (figure 4.2) and excavated a tomb,
noting the head at the south end, the absence of grave goods, and
the clay bricks covering the body (Clermont-Ganneau 1874: 81–3).
In 1903, E. W. G. Masterman visited wadi Qumran; he noted that
the graves and ruins offered field for speculation as to their origins,
and described a carefully built aqueduct running about half a mile
from its source where the wadi empties itself over the cliffs through
a rockcut channel and a tunnel to the ruins of Kh. Qumran.
Masterman saw the carefully constructed aqueduct, the road which
he discovered down the north side of the wadi, and the ruins of
nearby Kh. Abu Tabaq as evidence of a period when 'this now entirely
deserted corner of the Dead Sea was in no inconsiderable degree
inhabited', but he did not specify when (Masterman 1903: 267).
Gustav Dalman (1914: 9f.; 1920: 40) suggested that Kh. Qumran
was a Roman fort. In the Hebrew scriptures, Josh 15:61 lists six
cities of the Judaean wilderness: Beth-arabah, Middin, Secacah,
Nibshan, the City of Salt and Engedi. F.-M. Abel identifed Kh.
Qumran tentatively with Middin (1938, II, 386), Bar-Adon (1977:
22–3) identified it with Secacah, and Martin Noth (1938: 72) and
F. M. Cross (1956: 5–17) with the City of Salt. These identifications presupposed that Kh. Qumran was an Iron Age ruin, at least
at one stage of its career, and so indeed it turned out to be.

THE DISCOVERY OF THE SCROLLS

Kh. Qumran might never have been excavated had not shepherds
of the Ta'amireh tribe accidentally stumbled on some leather scrolls
in a cave north of Kh. Qumran in the winter of 1947–8 (for the
location of the caves, see figure 4.3). Even this find was not unprecedented. In the reign of Caracalla (211–17 CE) a Greek version of
the psalms together with other Greek and Hebrew manuscripts had
been found in a jar near Jericho, and in c. 785 CE books of the
Hebrew scriptures and other books in Hebrew writing were found
in a cave near Jericho (Milik 1959: 19, note). What happened to
these manuscripts we do not know. But when Mohammed ed-Dhib

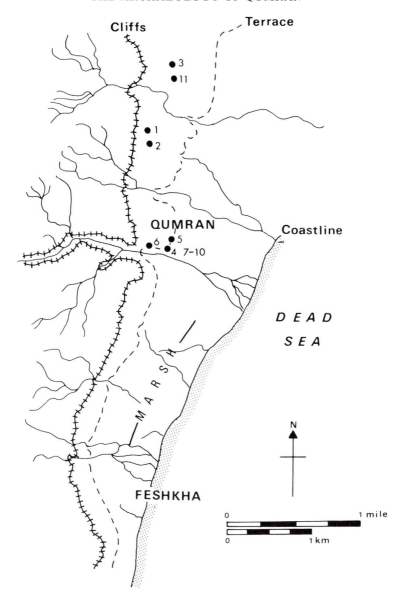

Figure 4.3 Map of Qumran area, showing Caves 1–11.
From Davies (1982).

explored what we now call Cave 1 and extracted three scrolls which soon found their way to a dealer in Bethlehem, he began a major industry which changed the lives of many scholars and others. Further excavation in the cave by the Bedouin brought to light four more scrolls; and of these seven, three were acquired by the Hebrew University (the War Scroll [1QM], the Hymn Scroll [1QH] and the second, fragmentary, Isaiah Scroll [IQIs.b]). The other four – 1QS (the Community Rule/Manual of Discipline), 1QIs.a, 1QpHab, 1QGenAp – were bought by the Syrian Metropolitan in Jerusalem, Mar Yeshue Samuel, who showed them to John Trevor and William Brownlee at the American School of Oriental Research in Jerusalem, and later sold them in America The actual adventures of these scrolls are not our present business, but their discovery and recognition as ancient Jewish documents began a serious search for more. The cave from which they came was found about 1 km north of Kh. Qumran by Arab Legion soldiers in January 1949 and systematically excavated by the Jordanian Department of Antiquities with the Ecole Archéologique and the Palestine Archaeological Museum between 15 February and 5 March 1949. They found Hellenistic/Roman period pottery and some linen, which was dated by the then newly discovered Carbon-14 technique to 33 CE (+/– 200); a first-century CE date was thus suggested, and confirmed by the style of the weaving, which suggested late first century.

The first cave was in the cliffs, and in February 1952 the Bedouin discovered a second cave. It contained only small fragments of scrolls, but in March the Palestine Archaeological Museum, the Ecole Archéologique, and the American School combined to clear it and explore the cliffs for 4–5 km north and south of Qumran. They examined 270 caves and crevices, finding twenty-six with pottery like that found in Cave 1; and they discovered Cave 3, which held fragments of hide, papyrus, thirty cylindrical jars of the kind in which the first scrolls had been discovered, and, its most important yield, a copper scroll in two parts. Meanwhile the bedouin had switched the search to the marl terraces. They made the important discovery of Cave 4, artificially hollowed out of the terraces opposite Kh. Qumran, and full of fragments of manuscripts, the remains of several hundred scrolls. This cave was professionally excavated in September 1952, when the excavators discovered Cave 5 nearby. Cave 6, containing a small wad of fragments, was found by the bedouin at the foot of a cliff. Caves 7–10 were discovered by the excavators in 1955 in the side of the marl terrace beneath Kh. Qumran; they contained only a few fragments of manuscripts. The final cave discovery was of Cave 11, discovered by the bedouin in 1956, with an important group of manuscripts (for example 11QMelch, a psalm scroll, a targum of Job, and perhaps originally the famous Temple Scroll). Thus Caves 1, 2, 3, 6, 11 were natural caves in the cliffs; Caves 4, 5, 7–10 were artificially hollowed out, probably originally for domestic habitation, in the marl terraces. The greatest manuscript discoveries were made in Caves 1, 3 (the copper scroll), 4 and 11; but pottery of the kind associated with the scrolls and identical with that found at Kh. Qumran was found in some twenty-six of the 270 caves examined.

THE OCCUPATION OF THE SITE

From a very early stage the scrolls were associated in the minds of many scholars with the Essenes, a Jewish group described at some length and in some detail by Josephus in the first century CE (*Jewish War* II.viii.2–13 [119–61]; *Antiquities* XIII.v.9 [171–2], XV.x.4–5 [371–9], XVIII.i.5 [18–22]). The Roman first-century author Pliny the Elder (Pliny published his *Natural History* in 77 CE, and died in 79 CE, caught in the famous eruption of Vesuvius which smothered Pompeii) described a group of Essenes living on the western shore of the Dead Sea, with palm trees alone for company, above Engedi (*Nat. Hist.* V.17.4 [73]). In fact Pliny said that Engedi lay 'infra', 'below', the Essene community, a phrase which has caused much debate, but it is generally accepted that Pliny meant that Engedi lay south of the Essenes rather than 'lower down the mountainside'. These connections led the archaeologists to turn again to examine Kh. Qumran with its aqueduct and its 'enigmatic' cemetery of some 1,100 graves. After a preliminary reconnaissance, Lankester Harding of the Jordanian Department of Antiquities and Roland de Vaux of the Ecole Biblique in Jerusalem made an initial sounding of the ruin in December 1951, and discovered pottery identical to that found in the caves (de Vaux 1953: 83–106). This was taken to reinforce the guess that the scrolls and caves were associated with Kh. Qumran, and led to the complete excavation of the site in four seasons from 1953–6.

De Vaux and his team found that the earliest building on the site (figure 4.4) was a courtyard with evidence of rooms on the north, east and south sides, with a smaller outbuilding on the west enclosing a round cistern. The associated pottery was Iron Age II; a stamped jar-handle inscribed 'for the king' and an ostracon in the early

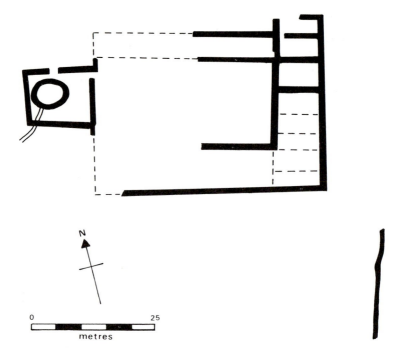

Figure 4.4 Plan of Qumran, Period I (seventh century BCE): courtyard with surrounding rooms and cistern to the west. From Davies (1982).

Hebrew script confirmed that this building probably belonged to the period between the ninth and seventh centuries BCE (de Vaux 1973: 1–3). F. M. Cross and J. T. Milik associated this building with similar buildings of about the same size in the Buqeah plain to the west, and with the list of cities 'in the wilderness' in Joshua 15.61; they were perhaps the work of the ninth-century king Jehoshaphat of Judah (*c.* 870–848 BCE; cf. 2 Chronicles 17:12) or the eighth-century king Hezekiah of Judah (*c.* 781–40 BCE; cf. 2 Chronicles 26:10) (Cross and Milik 1956: 5–17). This early building at Kh. Qumran was hardly a 'city' or even a village, but probably some sort of military garrison fort. The building was destroyed by fire, perhaps at the end of the Judaean monarchy. There is no reason to link this building with the scrolls.

The next occupation of the site, known as Period Ia, re-used the earlier building (now some six or seven hundred years old) by adding

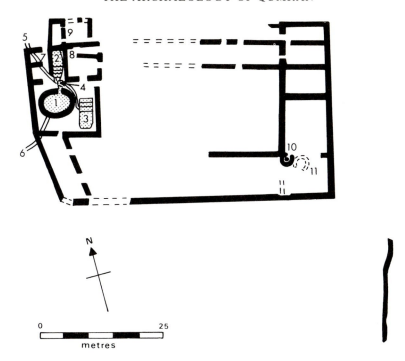

Figure 4.5 Plan of Qumran, Period Ia (second century BCE): water channel, rectangular cisterns, and potters' kiln added. From Davies (1982).

a water channel to collect water from the area north of the ruin, two rectangular cisterns and a decantation basin and some more rooms on the northwest side, and two potter's kilns in the eastern corner (figure 4.5). There seems to be virtually no dating evidence for this period, what little attributable pottery found being the same as that known from the following period Ib, which at least suggests that Ia and Ib were virtually continuous (de Vaux 1973: 3–5). But the concern for a water supply and the need to make pottery is also suggestive; people lived here in some organised form of society.

Period Ib (figure 4.6) saw a dramatic development in the site (de Vaux 1973: 5–24). Periods Ib and II constitute the main history of the settlement, whatever it was. The round cistern and the two associated rectangular cisterns remain. The site has been extended to the north by a large open courtyard and a decantation tank receiving water from an aqueduct coming from the wadi Qumran; west of

75

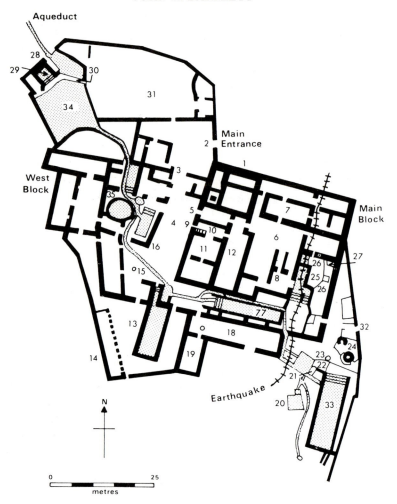

Figure 4.6 Plan of Qumran, Period Ib (first century BCE): major expansion, with tower (1), major rooms, and developed water system and cisterns. From Davies (1982).

the cisterns are new storerooms or workshops, and to the south of them in the corner of the outer wall what look like stables. Just south of the early cisterns are a flour mill and an oven. East of the earlier cisterns the main block has been developed; its north-west corner has become a solid tower (the ground-floor walls are more solid than other walls of the building, and apparently had no

76

windows or doors; access was from the first floor). The room opening onto the courtyard from the north was perhaps a kitchen. The south-western corner of the main complex is taken up with a small meeting room with a bench round it, and next door a long rectangular room (Davies 1982: 43 plan 3 no. 12; de Vaux 1973: plate xxxix no. 30) which may have been some sort of larger meeting or working room. On the eastern side of the courtyard are basins. In the south-east corner of the main complex a large new stepped cistern has been built. Stepped cisterns are a feature of this complex; from the old circular cistern the water channel goes south-east to service a new and large cistern, turns east for another stepped cistern on the south side of the main complex, and then divides to service both the new eastern cistern and the pottery makers, as well as another large stepped cistern at the very south-east corner of the complex. I suspect that this is the cistern seen by Clermont-Ganneau (1874: 82–3). On the south side of the complex, south of the cistern, lies a meeting or dining hall (no. 77 on de Vaux's plan; no. 18 on Davies's), with a pantry attached. This dining hall is conveniently close to the water system, and could apparently be washed out by a stream of water directed by sluices from the main channel.

The end of Period Ib is marked, according to de Vaux (1973: 21), by a fire in the buildings. The evidence for this lies in the ash deposits of burnt reed in the open spaces round the buildings (ash inside would have been cleaned out when the buildings were re-used in Period II). The major cracks in the cisterns on the east side of the building, the cracking of the eastern wall of the tower, and the collapse of the southern pantry wall burying a lot of pottery, have been taken to indicate that Period Ib was ended by an earthquake, and the most obvious candidate (though not the only candidate; the earthquakes of 64 BCE and 24 BCE have also been suggested) has been the earthquake described by Josephus as terrifying Herod's soldiers in the plains of Jericho in 31 BCE. However, it has also been suggested that it was not an earthquake that destroyed the eastern cisterns but the weight of water on the unstable marl Lisan below; other scholars have pointed out that the fire might have been quite independent of any earthquake (for more detailed discussion of the relationship between Periods Ib and II at Qumran see Callaway 1988: 44–9). Neither the destruction of a cistern nor the outbreak of fire need in themselves have caused any long break in occupation of the settlement. De Vaux argues that the waterlaid sediment found over-laying the ash in the courtyard on the north suggests a damaged

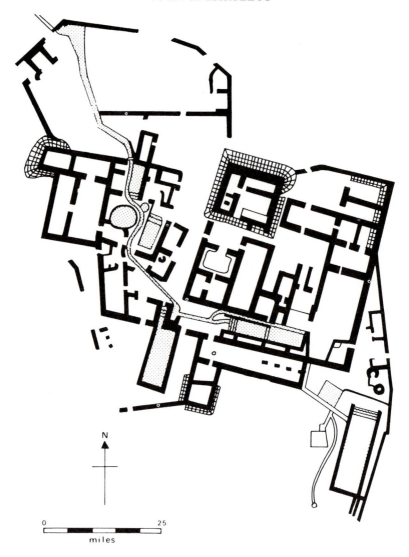

Figure 4.7 Plan of Qumran, Period II (first century BCE–first century CE):
buttressing added round tower, and other modifications.
From Davies (1982).

water-system and a period of abandonment. But there seems no suggestion that sediment from a major flood extended over the site as a whole, and 75 cm of sediment in part of this courtyard, which might have been deposited over a period of time if the decantation tank regularly overflowed, does not seem sufficient evidence to suggest any major break in occupation, evidence for which really depends on one's interpretation of the coinage found at the site. To this we shall return.

Period Ib was followed, at whatever interval, by Period II (figure 4.7). Major buttressing was added round the tower, and to the store-rooms at the north-west corner of the site, and to the pantry on the south. The north-east corner was modified. Various rooms were sub-divided. The main decantation basin went out of use and was replaced by a smaller one. The central cistern between the main block and the dining room/meeting room on the south was divided into two, and the former eastern cistern, cracked, went out of use. These changes are modifications rather than major structural alter-ations, and general working of the complex cannot have been much affected. Period II ended, according to de Vaux, with violent destruc-tion; iron arrowheads and evidence of burning and collapse of ceilings and superstructures suggest military action, and 'since the last coins of Period II are Jewish coins from the first revolt, it is reasonable to conclude that the destruction took place during the Jewish War' (de Vaux 1973: 36). De Vaux argues for June 68 CE, on the grounds that the last coins in Period II's stratigraphy are four Jewish coins from the third year of the revolt, and the earliest coins of Period III are Gentile coins of 67/8 CE from Caesarea and Dora, probably used by Roman soldiers. He agrees that the Jewish coins do not prove that the Jews left Qumran in 68 CE, and that the coins from Caesarea and Dora do not prove that the Romans installed themselves in 68 CE immediately after the expulsion of the Jews, but since the two groups of coins are distributed so precisely between the two successive levels, the obvious answer is the right one.

In Period III (figure 4.8) the site was considerably simplified. The western buildings, and even the cisterns, were abandoned, and a ditch dug along the west side. The tower was reinforced, and the water channel made to serve only the large south-eastern cistern (the one that Clermont-Ganneau found 1,800 years later). The potter's kiln became a store for lime. One bread oven was set up at the base of the tower. There is little pottery, and apart from one coin of Agrippa II from 87 CE, there are no coins after 72/3 CE.

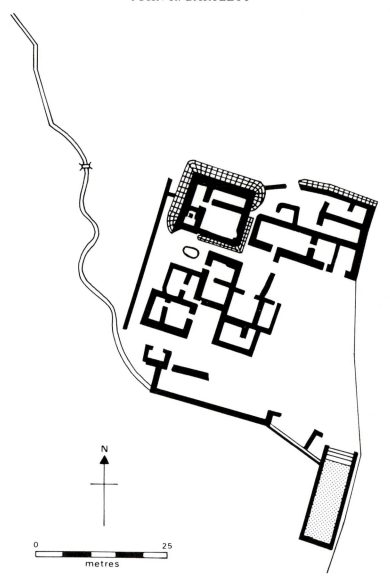

Figure 4.8 Plan of Qumran, Period III (late first century CE): Roman simplification. From Davies (1982).

De Vaux suggests that perhaps after the fall of Masada in 73 CE this military garrison was abandoned (de Vaux 1973: 44).

So much for the outlines of this ancient settlement; we can now turn to the more interesting questions. What dates can we ascribe to Periods Ia, Ib and II? What kind of settlement or building is this? What was the purpose of the elaborate water system? What are we to make of the use of certain rooms? What can be learned from the associated cemeteries? What do we make of the burials in various courtyards of animal bones? What is the relationship with the local caves? And what is the relationship with other nearby sites – 'Ain Feshka, 'Ain el-Ghuweir, Kh. el-Yahud, Kh. Mazin, Hiam el-Sagha, and others? And lastly, how should the archaeological evidence be related to the scrolls and their contents?

DATING

There is no certain evidence for Period Ia, which is distinguishable from Period Ib only with difficulty, and probably immediately precedes it. From Period Ib we have some silver coins from the years between 132 and 129 BCE (Antiochus VII) (which might have had a long life in circulation), one Jewish coin which might be ascribed to John Hyrcanus (if he minted coins), one of Aristobulus (104/3 BCE) (if he minted coins), 143 from Jannaeus (103–76 BCE), one from Salome and Hyrcanus II (76–67 BCE), five from Hyrcanus II (67, 63–40 BCE), four from Mattathias (40–37 BCE), and ten coins from Herod the Great (though from 'mixed levels', and therefore uncertain evidence for Period Ib). The bulk of the evidence is clearly from Jannaeus's reign, with some evidence for subsequent decades to the end of the century. There are sixteen coins of Herod Archelaus (4 BCE–6 CE), 'and

> from this point on the numismatic sequence of Period II continues uninterrupted. It includes ninety-one coins of the procurators (thirty-three of which were struck under Nero), and seventy-eight coins of Agrippa I (41–4 CE), and continues until the important group of coins belonging to the First Revolt'.
>
> (de Vaux 1973: 34)

It looks, on the face of it, as if Periods Ib and II can be dated from early in the first century BCE to 68 CE. The break between these two periods, if there is one, comes some time in Herod's reign, because a large hoard of 561 Tyrian silver coins, in three pots, with dates ranging from *c.* 116 to 9/8 BCE, was discovered dug into the Period II levels, but above the remains of Period Ib. Clearly this hoard was buried after 9/8 BCE, and probably before 1 BCE/1 CE, because no new Tyrian coins were issued between those years, and the hoard contains nothing after the turn of the era. If this hoard was buried after the beginning of Period II, Period II begins sometime in this decade, and for de Vaux, a coin of Herod Archelaus found in the debris of Period Ib cleared away for Period II confirms this dating. That is, Period II began in Archelaus's reign but before 1 BCE/1 CE. This could be right; but I see no reason to believe that there was any major break between the occupation of Periods Ib and II. The important evidence here must be the stratigraphy, not the coins or the cracked cistern.

If for the moment we assume a direct connection between the manuscripts found in the caves and the buildings of Kh. Qumran, the date of the manuscripts is important evidence. F. M. Cross (1993: 23) grouped the manuscripts on palaeographic grounds into three types:

1 a small group of 'archaic' biblical manuscripts from *c.* 250–150 BCE, all from Cave 4;
2 a large number of manuscripts from the Hasmonaean period; and
3 a group of manuscripts in 'Herodian' style, from *c.* 30 BCE–70 CE.

Philip Callaway refines this a little (1988: 199–200); he dates 1QS, 1QSa,b and 4QTest, all from the same hand, as from *c.* 100–75 BCE; CD from 75–50 BCE; and 1QpHab, 4QpNah, 4QpPs37, 1QM, 1QH as being copied in the Herodian period, these last being the documents that refer or allude to the history of the sect. The oldest copy of a sectarian document is thus dated to Jannaeus's time, and the younger copies of sectarian documents from Herod's reign. Recent radio-carbon dating of some of the manuscripts (Bonani and others 1991: 27–32) tends to support this general picture; thus some of the biblical manuscripts from Cave 4 are dated to the second century BCE (4Q365, 4QSam), and sectarian documents such as the Temple Scroll (11Q Temple) and the Genesis Apocryphon (1QApGen) to the first century BC, and 1QH to 21 BCE to 60 CE). If we could prove any of these to be autograph copies, of course, we would have some very significant dating evidence. But this work suggests that the group that copied these documents was active throughout the first century BCE and perhaps into the first century CE, and could be associated with Kh. Qumran's Period Ib–II. The import of their evidence for the early history of the group, perhaps in the second century BCE, is of course a matter for another lecture.

NATURE OF THE SETTLEMENT

De Vaux, identifying the occupants of Kh. Qumran as the Essenes mentioned by Pliny and Josephus, thought of the ruins as a monastic settlement. Many have criticised him for jumping too easily to conclusions based more on presuppositions than on evidence, and so referring to refectories and scriptoria more appropriate to a Christian monastery than to a first century BCE Jewish settlement, but, as S. Goranson (1991: 110–11) pointed out, the word *monasterion* first appears in Philo. The earliest settlement at Qumran may have had a military purpose; and P. Bar-Adon (1981: 349–52) thinks of Kh. Qumran Ia as a Hasmonaean fortress built by Hyrcanus, along with Qasr el-Yahud and Kh. Mazin. But Period Ib, with its greatly improved water system and its pottery and large rooms and stables and its extended grouping of buildings, seems to have had a wider purpose, even if the thicker-walled tower building suggests a certain amount of self-defence against casual raiders. Some have suggested that this was a villa, a well-watered residence, perhaps, or winter palace retreat from Jerusalem. The buildings, with their many stepped cisterns, might bear some comparison with the wealthy first-century CE house excavated in Jerusalem by Avigad, but there is little evidence of wealthy furnishings, unless the 'scriptorium' is a 'coenaculum' as Pauline Donceel-Voûte suggests (1992: 61–84), and little comparison with the Hasmonaean or Herodian villa in the Wadi Qelt.

PURPOSE OF THE WATER SYSTEM

The original Iron Age building or fortress obviously needed water for drinking purposes. B. G. Wood (1984: 45–60) asks why the builders of Period Ia, using the same ground plan, needed to increase the capacity so greatly, providing much more water than was needed for the normal requirements of life, and why full width steps were built into the cistern. Such wide steps reduce the capacity of the cistern, and one might expect narrow steps along one side. Period

Ia had two stepped cisterns and one unstepped cistern; Period Ib added a better water supply and more cisterns, ending up with five stepped, and two unstepped cisterns, together with small baths and industrial installations (for example for potters). Period II lost the use of the eastern cisterns but subdivided the large cistern (de Vaux locations 56/58 on plan, 1973, plate xxxix) along the southern side of the main block, creating a stepped cistern for ritual purposes and an unstepped one for functional purposes. Dividers were built at the top of the cistern steps, a device used for *miqva'oth*, to distinguish between unclean and clean, entrance and exit. In short, Kh. Qumran arranged its water supply for ritual purposes; or, conceivably, for industrial purposes of some kind demanding large quantities of water (one notes the large cistern complex at ʿAin Feshka). When the Romans took over in Period III, they had no need for such a complex water system and reduced it to one large cistern.

THE 'SCRIPTORIUM'

Kh. Qumran has become famous not least for its 'scriptorium', the upper chamber of de Vaux's locus 30 in which were found among the debris of Period II two inkwells and what de Vaux interpreted as tables and benches for scribes. The reconstruction of these benches and tables is well known. B. M. Metzger pointed out (1959: 509–15) that no one could ever sit on such benches at such a table; the shapes and heights were all wrong. Ancient scribes stood or sat on the ground; possibly they sat on these tables with their feet on the benches. Others have suggested (Poole and Reed 1961: 114–23) that the tables were surfaces for the preparation of skins, their slightly concave shape allowing for the tanning process; but that would be a very messy business, and the preparation of parchments for writing (as distinct from skins for other purposes) does not require tannin, but scraping and dehairing and stretching and rubbing with lime and pumice, which is a little easier to envisage. Pauline Donceel-Voûte from Louvain (1992: 61–84) has argued that the 'scriptorium' was a dining room (figure 4.9), the 'tables' being couches on which those attending a dinner in Hellenistic times lay while being waited on. The 'benches' were the podium, or a 'trottoir', for the couches. The shallow plaster tray with two circular depressions on its upper surface is construed as a stand for wine jars (figure 4.10). This ingenious idea is attractive until one asks whether such plaster benches would stand the weight or whether they are wide enough (half a

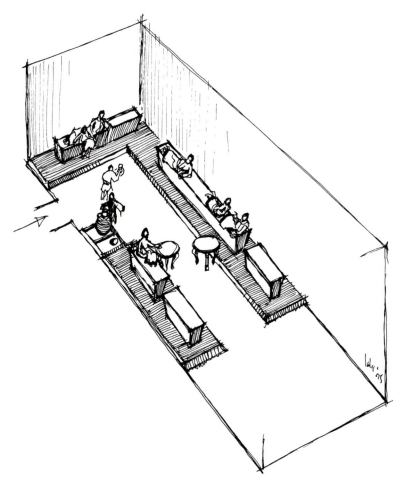

Figure 4.9 The 'coenaculum' as proposed by P. Donceel-Voûte. B. Lalor
after P. Donceel-Voûte (1992: 82, figure 12).

metre) to take a body comfortably. If the hypothesis were correct,
it would support the identification of Kh. Qumran as a villa of a
wealthy man rather than the home of an Essene group devoted to
an ascetic way of life. If Kh. Qumran is to be associated with the
scrolls in the local caves, the idea of a scriptorium remains an important possibility, even if the tables were used for purposes other than
writing.

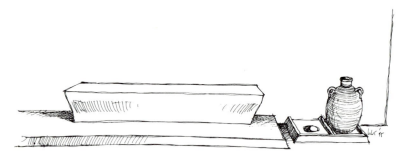

Figure 4.10 Couch, base and wine-jar stand as proposed by P. Donceel-Voûte. B. Lalor after P. Donceel-Voûte (1992: 67, figure 7).

ASSOCIATED CEMETERIES

De Vaux describes a vast cemetery of 1,100 graves in ordered rows and three main sections 50 m to the east of Kh. Qumran; it was first described by Clermont-Ganneau (1874: 83), who excavated one grave on 29 November 1873, and found beneath the oval surface mound of stones a pit about 1 m deep, at the bottom of which was a row of mudbricks covering the corpse, whose head lay to the south. There were no grave goods. De Vaux (1973: 45–7) excavated twenty-six tombs from different sectors of the cemetery, and corroborates this picture, though finding that the loculus at the bottom was a cavity dug into the side of pit. One rectangular grave contained a woman; four women and one child were found 'in the extensions of the cemetery over the hillocks to the east' (de Vaux 1973: 47), though S. H. Steckoll (1969: 33–40) sees the cemetery as one unified cemetery and believes that women and children were not an irregularity in it. Steckoll in 1966 opened a number of graves, and argued from deformations of the skeletons that one occupant was a scribe by profession, another a labourer who carried heavy weights on his shoulders (Steckoll 1968: 323–44); de Vaux caustically and perhaps a little unfairly remarked (1973: 48) that the Israeli authorities had forbidden this Sherlock Holmes of archaeology to continue his researches. The presence of women raises questions in the light of Pliny's remark that that the Essenes lived near the Dead Sea *sine ulla femina*, and Josephus's comment that the Essenes were mostly unmarried, but the Community Rule (1QSa) and the Cairo Damascus document (CD) imply that the Essenes were married and make no reference to celibacy. P. Bar-Adon excavated a similar cemetery 800 m north of 'Ain el-Ghuweir, some 15 km south of Qumran (1970: 398–400; 1977: 1–25); here out of twenty tombs excavated there were twelve males and seven females and one boy, all oriented north–south with heads to the south; N. Haas (1968: 345–53) noted that these people had been less healthy than their Qumran contemporaries. Hanan Eshel (1993: 252–9) excavated a similar cemetery at Hiam el-Sagha on the mountain between 'Ain el-Ghuweir and 'Ain et-Turaba, and noted that similar burials had been recorded at Jericho (C.-M. Bennett 1965: 514–46, espec. 537). Eshel suggested that such graves might be those of nomads living between the Wadi Murraba'at and Wadi Turaba, with a burial ideology similar to that of the Qumran sect. Yet the link between these places and Qumran remains unclear. N. Golb (1993: 53–7; 1985: 68–82) suggested that the burials at Qumran were the graves of troops killed defending the site, which he sees as a fortress; but such a carefully dug and well laid out cemetery seems unlikely for the losers in 68 CE; P. Bar-Adon (1981: 349–52) refined this by suggesting that the Qumran cemeteries were a central burial ground for military personnel occupying the Hasmonaean citadels or fortresses of the area, but there seems no positive evidence that these were the graves of soldiers, and M. Broshi (1992: 103–15 [113]) pointed out that it is unlikely that the Qumran people would co-operate with the Hasmonaean rulers, with whom there seems to have been mutual hostility.

BURIALS OF ANIMAL BONES

Also puzzling are the interments of collections of animal bones (never a whole skeleton), mostly of goat or sheep but occasionally of cows or calves, in cooking pots or jars in open spaces between buildings at Kh. Qumran. De Vaux (1973: 12–14) attributes thirty-three to Period Ib, and twenty-six to Period II. They perhaps represent the remains of meals (though some of the bones buried would not have had much flesh on them); they seem to have been treated in a special manner and so were presumably important; they were hardly seen as unclean or they would have been buried outside the buildings, so perhaps they were sacred in some way. There are not a great number; should one think of some annual ceremony, perhaps of covenant renewal? They do not seem to have been buried very deeply, so why have they survived? Laperrousaz (1978: 569–73) suggests that they are the remains of festival meals eaten outside the dining room/refectory by those not senior enough to have a seat there, and that the community was attacked on the feast day, and the meals left where they fell. This seems unlikely enough, but Laperrousaz hypothesises further that because such remnants are preserved from both Period Ib and Period II, the same thing happened twice, by coincidence, in 63 BCE (Pompey) and 68 CE (Vespasian). It may be coincidental, and not illogical (Laperrousaz 1978: 573), but it remains unlikely.

KHIRBET QUMRAN AND THE CAVES

What is the relationship between Kh. Qumran and the local caves? N. Golb (1993: 53–7) has denied that the scrolls found in the caves were written at Qumran, which was a fortress, not a monastery, and not to be identified with the location of the Essenes referred to by Pliny. The scrolls came from the heterogeneous collection in the Temple library at Jerusalem on the eve of the Roman siege of Jerusalem; they show various religious connections, and only a few can be said to reflect Essene ideas. The Qumran writings are not the work of a single sect, but the remnants of a large Jewish litera-ture. But Qumran makes a poor fortress, and probably is to be identified with the Essene site described by Pliny. The archaeolog-ical links between Kh. Qumran and the caves are secure – the same pottery from the same periods appears in both; Qumran has inkwells as evidence that writing was done there, whatever the tables were for – and it is hard to avoid the notion that a considerable amount of writing happened at Qumran (even if Qumran, with 600–800 manuscripts known from the caves, produced more than was strictly necesary for its own internal use) (Goranson 1991: 110–11).

ʿAIN FESHKA

About 2 km south of Kh. Qumran, where the mountains reach the Dead Sea, is the spring of Feshka, and just beside it a complex of buildings (figure 4.11). The main block of about 25 m by 20 m comprises a courtyard with surrounding rooms. To the south of it there is a long building or shed fronted by pillars, and to the north a water channel and set of basins or cisterns. The area was almost certainly used then as now for watering flocks of sheep and goats,

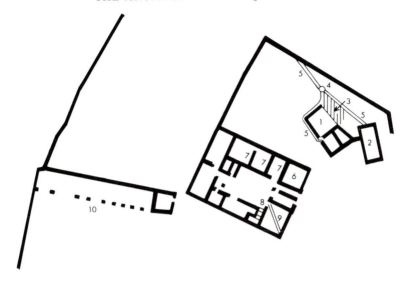

FESHKHA

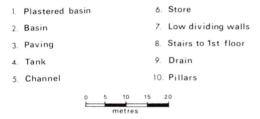

1. Plastered basin	6. Store
2. Basin	7. Low dividing walls
3. Paving	8. Stairs to 1st floor
4. Tank	9. Drain
5. Channel	10. Pillars

0   5   10   15   20
metres

Figure 4.11 Plan of 'Ain Feshka: roomed courtyard, with water channels and basins to the north. From Davies (1982).

and probably for growing dates and cutting the reeds which grew in the salt marshes. What the basins were used for is much debated. De Vaux (1973: 79–80) suggested a tannery, but no trace of hair or tannins has been found in the basin sediments, and F. E. Zeuner (1960: 27–36) suggests that these installations were used for fish farming. J. B. Poole and R. Reed (1961: 114–23) suggested the preparation of flax for linen; these basins would then be retting pits, but there is no material evidence for this. The problem remains unresolved. What is clear is that these buildings were in use contemporaneously with those of Periods Ib and II at Kh. Qumran. The

JOHN R. BARTLETT

architecture is similar, the pottery and coinage basically the same. De Vaux distinguishes two periods of occupation at Feshka as at Kh. Qumran, but there is no sign of any fire or earthquake damage at Feshka between them; they can be distinguished only by secondary modifications to the building and some piles of discarded rubble apparently cleared out of the building at some stage. The evidence of a gap in occupation is even less secure here than at Kh. Qumran. The second period ended, however, as at Kh. Qumran, with fire and was followed, as at Kh. Qumran, by a third period of occupation at the end of the first century or early in the second, perhaps during the Jewish Revolt of 132–5 CE.

OTHER NEARBY ARCHAEOLOGICAL SITES

We should finally mention the other archaeological sites in the region of Kh. Qumran, sites which may have been related in some way. P. Bar-Adon excavated a building 43 m by 19.5 m with a hall, kitchen, and store rooms at ʿAin el-Ghuweir, 15 km south of Qumran on the Dead Sea shore (Bar-Adon 1977: 1–25). Coins found suggested its occupation under Herod, Archelaus and Agrippa I; the pottery was typical first century BCE/CE. Eight hundred metres north was the cemetery of the Qumran type already mentioned (de Vaux 1973: 88–9). Two kilometres to the south-west Hanan Eshel (1993: 252–9) excavated another similar cemetery, Hiam el-Sagha. One kilometre south of Kh. Qumran itself de Vaux explored a large building 60 m by 64 m, perhaps originally from the Iron Age; this is probably the barely distinguishable square enclosure noted by de Saulcy (1853: II. 63) just south of Kh. Qumran. De Saulcy also noted and described Kh. el-Yahud (= Kh. Mazin) south of ʿAin Feshka (1853: II. 58); its foundations were ʿof enormous blocks of unhewn stone, forming . . . cyclopean walls, a yard in thickness'. It appears, from de Saulcy's description, to have consisted of a courtyard with pavilions 6 yards square at intervals around it. P. Bar-Adon (1981: 349–52) mentions this site, identifying it as another Hasmonaean fortress built by Hyrcanus, together with Rujm el-Bahr north of Qumran. De Vaux, however, dated this rectangular building to the Roman period, tentatively associating it with the salt trade of the Dead Sea (de Vaux 1973: 88). Thus, to sum up, while those buried at el-Ghuweir and Hiam el-Sagha may have had some connection with the people of Kh. Qumran, sharing the same burial rites, other connections are much less clear; the building at ʿAin el-Ghuweir

90

might have provided for the needs of a group similar to those at Qumran. However, it should be noted that it is only at Qumran and in caves to the immediate north of Qumran that scrolls were found; there is no certainty that the people of Qumran were active south of 'Ain Feshka, unless one locates Pliny's Essenes immediately above Engedi rather than north of Engedi.

ARCHAEOLOGY AND INTERPRETATION OF THE SCROLLS

I have deliberately kept to the archaeological evidence, for that was my brief, but it is time to mention some of the major problems of the relationship of the archaeological findings to the fact and contents of the scrolls, in the hope that subsequent research will throw light on them. The archaeological evidence by itself is reasonably clear and straightforward; there are problems like the precise dating of the beginning of Periods Ia, Ib and II at Kh. Qumran, the precise function of certain rooms at Kh. Qumran, and the implications of the cemetery for the population of Qumran. But we should note how tempting it is to let the contents of the scrolls, and more particularly one's favoured interpretation of those scrolls, influence one's interpretation of the ruins. Those who want to connect the Wicked Priest of the scrolls with either Jonathan or Simon Maccabee would like to push the foundation of Kh. Qumran Ia back into the second century BCE; those who want to disconnect the scrolls from Kh. Qumran interpret de Vaux's locus 30 as a coenaculum rather than a scriptorium. The big question, therefore, is the relationship of Kh. Qumran with the caves and the literature found in them. Was the literature produced and copied by the people who occupied Kh. Qumran, or did it come from elsewhere, for example the Temple library? The fact that the scrolls are associated with pottery jars apparently made at Qumran does not prove that the Qumran people did more than make the pottery for them; but the evidence of inkwells at Qumran, and the fact that the scrolls were concealed in caves apparently occupied by the Qumran people, does make the obvious solution the most likely. If that is the case, what can the scrolls tell us about Kh. Qumran and its occupants? Perhaps strangely, the literature does not mention Kh. Qumran by name (unless some such code name as 'Damascus' is used), though the reference to the Teacher of Righteousness's place of exile may refer to Qumran. The literature probably tells us more (however cryptically) about the history of one particular group of Jews than it does about the particular history of Kh. Qumran; for that we have to base ourselves firmly on the archaeological evidence and not be misled by less substantial hypotheses. If Kh. Qumran was the home of a group or sub-group of the Essenes, the site began its Essene life not earlier than about 100 BCE, and it probably ended in 68 CE. This fits well with the dating given by other means for the sectarian documents, the oldest, 1QS, probably being written *c.* 100–75 BCE. But from this point we are in the hands of the textual critics and the literary critics and the historians.

BIBLIOGRAPHY

Abel, F.-M. (1938), *Géographie de la Palestine* I, II, Paris: Librairie Lecoffre.
Bar-Adon, P. (1970), 'Chronique archéologique', *RB* 77, 398–400.
—— (1977), 'Another settlement of the Judaean desert at 'En-el-Ghuweir on the shores of the Dead Sea', *BASOR* 227, 1–25.
—— (1981) 'The Hasmonaean fortresses and the status of Kh. Qumran', *EI* 15, 349–52 (Hebrew).
Barthelemy, D. and Milik, J. T. (1955) *Discoveries in the Judaean Desert of Jordan, I. Qumran Cave 1*, Oxford: Clarendon Press.
Bennett, C.-M. (1965) 'Tombs of the Roman period', in K. M. Kenyon (ed.) *Excavations at Jericho II: The tombs excavated in 1956–58*, London: British School of Archaeology in Jerusalem, 516–31.
Blake, I. M. (1966) 'Chronique archéologique: Rivage occidental de la Mer Morte', *RB* 73, 564–6.
—— (1967) 'Dead Sea sites of "the utter wilderness"', *ILN* 4 March, 27–9.
Bonani, G., Broshi, M., Carmi, I., Ivy, S., Strugnell, J. and Wolfli, W. (1991) 'Radio-carbon dating of the Dead Sea Scrolls', *Atiqot* 20: 27–32.
Broshi, M. (1992) 'The archaeology of Qumran – a reconsideration', in D. Dimant and V. Rappaport (eds) *The Dead Sea Scrolls: Forty years of research*, Guildford: Lutterworth, 103–15.
Callaway, P. R. (1988) *The History of the Qumran Community: An investigation*, JSPSup 3, Sheffield: JSOT.
Clermont-Ganneau, C. (1874) 'Letters from M. Clermont-Ganneau III', *PEFQS* 6, 81–3.
Cross, F. M. (1956) 'Explorations in the Judaean Buqê'ah', *BASOR* 142, 5–17.
—— (1993) 'The historical context of the Scrolls', in H. Shanks (ed.) *Understanding the Dead Sea Scrolls*, London: SPCK.
Cross, F. M. and Milik, J. T. (1956) 'Explorations in the Judaean Buqê'ah', *BASOR* 142, 5–17.
Davies, P. R. (1982) *Qumran: Cities of the biblical world*, Guildford: Lutterworth.
—— (1988) 'How not to do archaeology: the story of Qumran', *BA* 51(4), 203–7.
—— (1992) 'The pre-history of the Qumran community', in D. Dimant and U. Rappaport (eds) *The Dead Sea Scrolls: Forty years of research*,

Leiden: Brill; Jerusalem: Magnes Press; Jerusalem: Y. ben Zvi.

Donceel-Voûte, Pauline H. E. (1992) "Coenaculum" – la salle à l'étage du locus à 30 Khirbet Qumrân sur la Mer Morte', *Res Orientales* 4, 61–84.

Duhaime, J. L. (1977) 'Remarques sur les dépôts d'ossements d'animaux à Qumrân', *RevQ* 9, 245–51.

Eshel, Hanan (1993) 'Hiam el-Sagha, a cemetery of the Qumran type, Judaean desert', *RB* 100, 252–9.

Golb, N. (1985) 'Who hid the Dead Sea Scrolls?', *BA* 48, 68–82.

—— (1987) 'Réponse a la "Note" de E.-M. Laperrousaz', *Annales* 6, 1313–20.

—— (1993) 'Hypothesis of Jerusalem origin of DSS – synopsis', in Z. J. Kapera (ed.) *Mogilany 1989: Papers on the Dead Sea Scrolls offered in Memory of Jean Carmignaca*, I, 53–7.

—— (1990) 'Khirbet Qumran and the manuscripts of the Judaean wilderness: observations on the logic of their investigation', *JNES* 49, 103–14.

Goranson, S. (1991) 'Further Qumran archaeology publications in progress', *BA* 54(2), 110–11.

Josephus, Loeb Classical Library, vols I–IX, (1926–55) ed. H. St. J. Thackeray, R. Marcus, A. Wikgren and L. H. Feldman, London: Heinemann; Cambridge, Mass.: Harvard University Press.

Khairy, N. I. (1980) 'Inkwells of the Roman period from Jordan', *Levant* 12, 155–62.

Laperrousaz, E.-M. (1978), 'A propos des dépôts d'ossements d'animaux trouvés à Qumran', *RevQ* 9, 569–73.

—— (1987) 'Note sur l'origine des manuscrits de la Mer Morte', *Annales* 6, 1305–12.

Masterman, E. W. G. (1903) 'Notes on some ruins and a rockcut aqueduct in the wady Kumran', *PEFQS* 35, 267.

Metzger, B. M. (1959) 'The furniture in the scriptorium at Qumran', *RevQ* 1, 509–15.

Milik, J. T. (1959) *Ten Years of Discovery in the Wilderness of Judaea*, London: SCM Press.

Pliny, Loeb Classical Library, (1969) ed. H. Rackham, London: Heinemann; Cambridge, Mass.: Harvard University Press.

Poole, J. B. and Reed, R. (1961) 'The "tannery" of 'Ain Feshka', *PEQ* 93, 114–23.

de Saulcy, F. (1853) *Narrative of a Journey round the Dead Sea and in the Bible Lands in 1850 and 1851*, Vols I & II, London: Bentley.

Schiffman, L. H. (1993) 'The Sadducean origin of the Dead Sea Scrolls sect', in H. Shanks (ed.) *Understanding the Dead Sea Scrolls*, London: SPCK.

Sellers, O. R. (1951) 'Radio-carbon dating of cloth from the 'Ain Feshka cave', *BASOR* 123, 24–6.

Sharabani, M. (1980) 'Monnaies de Qumrân au Musée Rockefeller de Jérusalem', *RB* 87, 274–84.

Steckoll, S. H. (1968) 'Preliminary excavation report in the Qumran cemetery', *RevQ* 6, 323–44.

—— (1969) 'Marginal notes on the Qumran excavations', *RevQ* 7, 33–40.

Stegemann, H. (1992) 'The Qumran Essenes – local members of the main

Jewish union in Late Second Temple times', in J. T. Barrera and L. V. Montaner (eds) *The Madrid Qumran Congress: Proceedings of the International Congress on the Dead Sea Scrolls, Madrid 18–21 March, 1991,* I, 83–166, Leiden: Brill.

VanderKam, J. C. (1993), 'The people of the Dead Sea Scrolls: Essenes or Sadducees?', in H. Shanks (ed.) *Understanding the Dead Sea Scrolls,* London: SPCK.

de Vaux, R. (1953) 'Fouille au Khirbet Qumrân', *RB* 60, 83–106.

—— (1973) *Archaeology and the Dead Sea Scrolls,* London: Oxford University Press for the British Academy.

Wise, M. (1986) 'The Dead Sea Scrolls. Part 1. Archaeology and biblical manuscripts', *BA* 49(3), 140–54.

Wood, B. G. (1984) 'To dip or sprinkle? The Qumran cisterns in perspective', *BASOR* 256, 45–60.

Zeuner, F. E. (1960) 'Notes on Qumran', *PEQ* 92, 27–36.

5

THE TEMPLE MOUNT OF HEROD THE GREAT AT JERUSALEM

Recent excavations and literary sources

Brian Lalor

Vitruvius in his architectural treatise (dedicated to Augustus, therefore representative of contemporary thought in the first century BCE), while discussing the education of architects, defines the basis from which the subject must be approached:

> In all matters, but particularly in architecture, there are these two points: – the thing signified, and that which gives it its significance. That which is signified is the subject of which we may be speaking; and that which gives significance is a demonstration on scientific principles. It appears, then, that one who professes himself an architect should be well versed in both directions.
>
> (*De architectura* I. 1–3, trans. Morgan)

No contemporary text bears so pertinently on some of the problems of interpretation surrounding Herod's Temple Mount. 'That which is signified' is the site itself; the 'demonstration on scientific principles' underlying it represents the intellectual bias as well as the technical and stylistic repertoire of the designers of the complex. For present-day commentators the latter points are an area of considerable difficulty. The writings of Vitruvius should alert those involved in any study of the site to the fact that it can not be understood alone as the site of the Jewish Temple, but must be evaluated in the context of the most advanced architectural thinking of its period, a factor generally obscured by considerations of the site's cultic significance. Not only have recent excavations revealed the physical framework of the areas surrounding the Temple Mount, but they

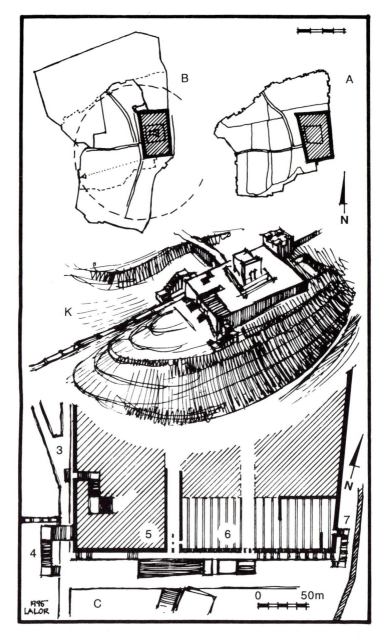

Figure 5.1 The Temple Mount in Jerusalem

have also enabled this information to be applied analytically to the Mount itself. It is only through a deeper understanding of the anatomy of the Temple Mount that the major problems concerning the location of the Temple and the purpose of its precincts may be better understood.

THE TEMPLE MOUNT

The Temple Mount in Jerusalem (figure 5.1: A) is a rectangular artificial platform, measuring 280 m by 488 m, enclosing an area of about 18 hectares, and located at the south-east corner of the present walled Old City, of which it forms a portion of the south and east perimeter, and comprises one-sixth of its total area. At its period of maximum development in the late first century CE (figure 5.1: B), the city stretched from the Tombs of the Kings in the north, to the Siloam Pool in the south, its eastern and western boundaries being an extension of the lines of today: Jerusalem was then approximately twice the size of the present walled city.

Figure 5.1 The Temple Mount in Jerusalem

A The Old City of Jerusalem today, within its largely sixteenth-century walls. The principal north–south and east–west routes, from the Damascus and Jaffa Gates, in part represent the line of the Herodian streets.

B The street which runs parallel to the Western Wall of the Temple Mount from the Antonia Fortress in the north and which proceeds south to the Lower City became defunct following the destruction of the Temple. The radius of the 'place of the trumpeting' does not include the area enclosed by the (late) Third Wall to the north, begun under Agrippa I, 41–4 CE.

K Aerial view of the Temple Mount viewed from the south-east, emphasising its topographical separation from the Upper City (left) and Kidron Valley (right). The Temple and Antonia Fortress are schematically represented. The drawing shows the Temple platform prior to the erection of the Basilica on the south and the porticoes on the north, east and west.

C There is a striking contrast between the void of the Triple Gate Undercroft and the apparently solid area betwen the Double Gate and the Western Wall. The centring of the columns of the Basilica which stood above the Double Gate and Undercroft must be dictated by the positions of the walls surviving in these areas. Access between the individual vaults of the Undercroft may have been as in the second-century CE Hadrianic roofing of the Strouthion Pool, by transverse arches – their function was most probably storage. This would be a conventional plan for store rooms, as in Masada. The Undercroft plan as presented here is a maximalist interpretation; a minimalist view would follow the current plan of Solomon's Stables. The Eastern Arch presents the problem of whether it was within or outside the city; its pier could conceivably have been the city–wall itself. The planning parallels between Robinson's Arch (4) and Barclay's Gate (2) are obvious.

97

Topographically, the Temple Mount sits on the brow of a natural ridge, Mt Moriah (figure 5.1: K), to the east of which is the 60-metre depth of the Kidron valley, while to the west and north are the rising ground of the current Jewish and Muslim Quarters. On the south, the land falls away gradually to the Ophel and towards the Siloam Pool. The form of the Mount today is an accretion of building and rebuilding dating from the eighth century BCE to the nineteenth century CE, with much of the body of evidence for what previously existed either beyond the scope of archaeological investigation due to the Temple platform being a holy place, or confined to the perimeter and substructures of the site. The fact that at best only fragmentary evidence of its original function as the location of the Solomonic temple and later as one of the most ambitious public works building projects of the classical world – the forum, cult place and centre of Jerusalem as built by Herod the Great (ruled 37 BCE–4 CE) – does not preclude it from being the source of rewarding study.

The life span of the Herodian buildings was less than a century, begun in *c.* 20 BCE and completed *c.* 20 CE (the literary sources differ on the lengths of time for construction, but this can easily be accounted for by whether 'the Temple' refers to the building itself or the entire project), although construction and repair continued after that date under Herod's successors. The entire complex was destroyed in 70 CE, by the combined action of the First Jewish Revolt and by the subsequent siege and destruction of the city by the Roman legions under Titus. The concern of this chapter is with the southern area of the Temple Mount, the precinct and environs of the Temple, rather than with the Temple itself, on which archaeology has so far cast no direct light. I deal only with the first-century BCE/first-century CE Herodian strata from the excavations, and associated observations in unexcavated areas.

Excavations

The excavations with which I am primarily concerned are those carried out by the Hebrew University/Israel Exploration Society at the western and southern walls of the Temple Mount and directed by Professor Benjamin Mazar between 1968 and 1977. Earlier and concurrent excavations which bear significantly upon the topic are the pioneering investigations of Warren and Wilson in the 1860s in the whole area of the Temple Mount; the work of Bliss and Dickie (1894–7) to the south; Kenyon and de Vaux for the British School of Archaeology and Ecole Biblique in 1961–7, in the immediate area of Mazar's excavations; Avigad's excavations for the Hebrew University/Israel Exploration Society, 1969–79, in the adjacent Jewish Quarter, as well as Bahat's excavations from 1985 along the Western Wall on behalf of the Ministry of Religious Affairs.

Literary sources

Any analysis of the character, function and detail of the Temple Mount leans heavily upon the fortunately abundant literary sources, for without this documentation only a very limited understanding of what stood on the Temple platform would be possible. Conversely, without dependence upon the literary information, an exacting study of the precincts and under-structure of the site from an archaeological and architectural point of view has independently yielded a wealth of important information which must now be regarded as fundamental to any future discussion of the religious nature of the site and the buildings which occupied it in its final century of use as the focal point of Judaism.

The literary sources reflect the centrality of the Temple Mount to first-century and later Judaism, as well as its importance to Christianity, with an abundance of references to be found in the writings of Flavius Josephus, the Synoptic Gospels and the Mishnah. These sources of information and commentary may be divided into two categories, the first encompassing Jewish and Christian religious sources, the second relating solely to Josephus. The difference relates to the dating and purpose of the two bodies of texts and the educational and cultural status and intention of their authors. The Mishnah is concerned with the interpretation of the Law and with the recording of religious practices in the Temple, and it preserves in minute detail much information concerning priestly rituals. The Gospels more briefly record events which took place in or around the Temple, but to which it forms no more than a backdrop. The authors of these texts were not primarily interested in architecture or topography *per se*, which places the commentaries and descriptions of Flavius Josephus, writing as a classical historian, in a uniquely authoritative position as a source on the physical nature of first-century Judaea. A comparison of Josephus' texts on Gamla, Jerusalem and Jotapata demonstrate his reliability as geographer and topographer, his physical descriptions being as valid today as when they were written.

The controversy which has surrounded Josephus' behaviour during the siege of Jotapata/Yodefat, afterwards in Jerusalem, and his later life in Rome as a protégé of the Flavian dynasty has no bearing on his reliability as a commentator on landscape and architecture. For this reason, the value of Josephus' sustained architectural narrative of the Temple Mount quite outweighs the relevance of information derived from all other sources and it is primarily the textual contribution of Josephus to the understanding of Herodian Jerusalem that the literary aspect of this chapter is concerned with. Josephus' commentary, unlike all other literary sources is contemporary and first-hand and, most significantly, since he was writing in first century CE Rome, Josephus would have been conversant with the architectural thought and practice of the period, at its very centre.

This question of thought and practice is of the utmost significance in evaluating the construction of the Temple Mount, for the results of Mazar's excavations demonstrate unequivocally that a combination of conceptual thoroughness, technical sophistication, superb craftmanship and immense financial resources were united in the creation of Herod's Temple Mount. The hyperbole of some of Josephus' language appears more reasonable in the light of hard archaeological evidence. In order to successfully anatomise the Temple Mount it is necessary to intellectually deconstruct it. Archaeology has made this exercise possible.

The history of the site prior to Herod's great work must be passed over in this study, although the fact that his building project is an extension and elaboration of what existed means that the pre-Herodian nature of the site cannot be ignored. Also, certain areas of the current Temple Mount are those which Herod's engineers incorporated into their building scheme, and these cast light upon the prior history of the area.

WESTERN AND SOUTHERN WALLS

Warren and his contemporaries identified the principal visible features of the Temple Mount, and all subsequent investigations have relied heavily upon these initial findings. In the years following 1968, the area south of the Western Wall prayer area was excavated by Mazar to the level of and below the Herodian streets flanking the Mount, revealing what can now be understood as one of the most complex examples of first-century BCE town planning to be found anywhere in the classical world, and also vindicating what were previously regarded as ambiguities in Josephus' text. It is worth quoting in full Josephus on the western and southern walls of the Temple Mount.

> Now, in the western quarter of the enclosures of the temple there were four gates; the first led to the king's palace, and went to a passage over the intermediate valley, two more led to the suburbs of the city; and the last led to the other city, where the road descended down into the valley by a great number of steps, and thence up again by the ascent; for the city lay over-against the temple in the manner of a theatre and was encompassed with a deep valley along the entire south quarter.
>
> (*Antiquities* XV. xi. 5 [Whiston])

These four gates on the west have been identified and named after their nineteenth-century discoverers or publicists, respectively following the order in the above text: Wilson's Arch, Warren's Gate, Barclay's Gate and Robinson's Arch (figure 5.2: F, nos 1–4). The last mentioned falls within the scope of Mazar's excavations. Identification of Robinson's Arch in the nineteenth century, its excavation in the 1960s, followed by evaluation and reconstruction provide the data that enable a detailed examination of a specific text and its illumination by recent archaeological excavation. The gates in the middle of the southern wall also fall within the area under discussion, and their function is clarified by reference to the archaeological evi-dence, the texts, and the study of these gates from within the Temple Mount.

Robinson's Arch

One of the major goals of the initial years' excavations was to clarify the character and significance of the structure known as Robinson's Arch (figure 5.1: C; figure 5.2: F, no. 4), believed since the mid-nineteenth-century investigations to be the remains of a great bridge spanning the Tyropoeon valley between the Temple Mount and the Upper City (despite the fact that Josephus' description cited above is not consistent with that interpretation). Robinson's Arch comprises an immense 15-metre-broad springing carried on impost blocks in the Herodian courses of the Western Wall, and, facing it across a 12-metre-wide split-level paved street, the corresponding pier of this arch. Between the wall and pier in the debris from the destruction of the Temple precinct are arch voussoirs, a keystone, the upper

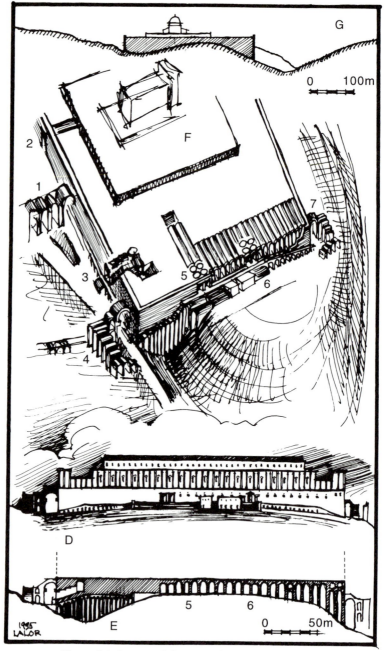

Figure 5.2 Structural features of the Temple Mount

section of a lugged Doric doorcase and many fragments of impost blocks from the pier, as well as limestone steps, polished from use. Excavation at appropriate intervals to the west of the pier had established that if further piers of this presumed bridge had existed, no evidence of them was now visible. What was actually revealed by excavating to the west of the pier was a complex of walls of smaller dimensions, enclosing plastered pools, most probably *miqva'oth* for ritual bathing. South of this area, a further series of parallel walls was revealed, at right angles to the street, some supporting the springing of vaults. In the elucidation of the significance of these remains lay the answer to the enigma of Robinson's Arch.

In order to pursue this question it is necessary to look at the entire southern area of the Temple Mount (figure 5.2: D) for an understanding of the actual significance of Robinson's Arch, its relationship to the planning considerations of its Herodian designers and to the text of Josephus. The *Antiquities* text continues:

> but the fourth front of the temple, which was southward, had indeed itself gates in its middle and had over it the Royal Portico, which had three aisles, extending in length from the eastern to the western ravine. It was not possible for it to extend further. And it was a structure more noteworthy than any under the sun . . .
>
> (*Antiquities* XV. xi. 5 [411–12])

Figure 5.2 Structural features of the Temple Mount

D Viewed from the south, the Basilica dominates the Lower City and was the most classically formal external aspect of the Temple Mount.

E From the south-west corner of the Mount (on the left), the narrow street running east–west and paralleling the southern wall is carried on arches supported by walls on bedrock in the depth of the Tyropoean Valley – a remarkable expenditure of effort to achieve such a simple purpose. The exact design of the Triple Gate Undercroft vaulting (right) is open to more than one interpretation.

F Collectively, the various uses of arches, vaults and domes is here demonstrated as a consistent response to the structural demands of the site.

G An east–west section through the Temple Mount, showing its relationship to the Kidron Valley, and the Dome of the Rock occupying the position of the Temple.

The Basilica

Of the Royal Portico or Basilica (*stoa basileos* in Josephus' text) and its platform nothing remains. Its former position and proportions as outlined by Josephus can be compared with Vitruvius' requirements for this type of building, indicating significant divergence.

> Basilicas should be constructed on a site adjoining the forum and in the warmest possible quarter, so that in winter businessmen may gather in them without being troubled by the weather. In breadth they should be not less than one third nor more than one half of their length, unless the site is naturally such as to prevent this and to oblige an alteration in these proportions.
>
> (*De architectura* V: 1, 4, trans. Morgan)

The site did not necessarily demand a departure from the proportions which he recommends, yet it is not easy to accommodate the idea of a building 'extending in length from the eastern to the western ravine', with Vitruvius' recommendations. Various textual references to towers at the corners, 'the Temple Chambers', etc., have prompted a compromise solution of a longer than normal basilica, yet not occupying the entire span of the southern wall. Such a cavalier approach to Josephus' text may be unwise. Without further information, the conflict on this issue between Josephus and Vitruvius is difficult to resolve.

The Double Gate

The understructures of the basilica, however, can be studied (Figure 5.1: C; figure 5.2: E) even though the superstructure is missing. The underpasses (nos 5 and 6) which gave access to the Temple courts from the concourse level below in the area of the excavations are still in existence, their entrances known today as the Double and Triple Gates. The former, to the west, survives largely intact, with a columned and elliptically domed vestibule and a vaulted 11-metre-wide passageway. These stone domes, decorated with contemporary stuccoed patterns, are early examples of domes on pendentives (a system by which the circular dome is accommodated to the rectangular arched and columnar support); the stucco treatment of the domes is articulated separately from the pendentives, confirming this understanding. This double doorway, leading to or from the Temple platform from a 65-metre-wide external stairway, is larger than that to the east and, perhaps significantly, stylistically different. The Mishnah (*Middoth* 1:3; see Danby 1933), in a reference to 'The two Hulda gates on the south, that served for coming in and going out', is presumably referring to these entrances (figure 5.2: F, nos 5 and 6). In classical architecture a duality is anathema, entrances being invariably singular or triple, maintaining the principles of axial symmetry. The duality of the Double Gate, as well as its lack of external ornament, must reflect on its functional purpose as such details are unlikely to be arbitrary (the fact that internally the vestibule is the most richly ornamented surviving fragment of the entire Temple Mount is in itself an intriguing question). The positioning of both gates in the southern wall of the Temple Mount also represents a duality, in this case an asymmetric one, perhaps dictated by the internal criteria of the Temple Mount and the pre-Herodian plan.

Triple Gate undercroft

Of the Triple Gate entrance, only the base course of the *cyma reversa* doorcase moulding is in place. Internally the arcaded Crusader structure to which it leads, now known as Solomon's Stables, has preserved within it important remains of the vaulted Herodian support for the original platform in the form of vault springings. It is possible that the function of the Herodian Triple Gate was primarily as entrance to this undercroft rather than a pilgrim entrance (figure 5.1: C), although the Mishnah (*Middoth* 2:2) suggests it as the entrance, with the Double Gate as the exit: 'All who enter to the Temple Mount enter by way of the right and go round and exit by way of the left.' The smallness of its external flight of steps (15 m) also emphasises the distinction. It is of interest to divide up the Gates on a stylistic basis, Barclay's Gate and the Double Gate being unadorned, Robinson's Arch and the Triple Gate having decoration.

The Eastern Arch

On the eastern wall of the Temple Mount, 20 m north of the southeast corner, is an arch springing corresponding to Robinson's Arch, but smaller in width and some 15 m lower (figure 5.1: C, no. 7; figure 5.2: F, no. 7). It gave access to the undercroft below the eastern section of the Royal Portico, contained between the south and east walls and the Double Gate passageway from which there is also an

existing entrance. Warren probed for the pier of this eastern arch –
as he had successfully done for that of Robinson's Arch – but without
success; no excavation has taken place here subsequently.

In 1971, after extensive study of the evidence, I advanced the
proposition that as the eastern arch was unlikely to represent a Pont
du Gard style bridge spanning the 60-metre-deep and 200-metre-
wide Kidron Valley (figure 5.2: G), it must in fact represent some
quarter-turn or dog-leg type of descending ramp or stepped access,
and that Robinson's Arch might possibly be also explained in this
manner. It remained for the archaeological evidence to sustain or
refute this interpretation.

The southern wall of the Temple Mount, viewed from the Lower
City, with the Royal Stoa occupying the whole southern range ('It
was not possible for it to extend further', figure 5.2: D), presented
a classical composition which was augmented by flanking arches
(although of different sizes, dictated by different functions), with the
clear architectural intention of presenting a balanced southern elevation. Explication of the nature of these attendant 'flying buttresses'
depended on the fruits of excavation, none being possible on the
eastern side due to the proximity of a cemetery. The burden of proof
rests on what might be achieved in the west.

Solution of Robinson's Arch

A study of the architectural fragments in the destruction levels
between Robinson's Arch and its pier concentrated attention on the
existence of large numbers of two-stepped ashlars. These seemed to
indicate that whatever rested upon the arch was stepped in some
manner. Now when we turn our attention to the series of parallel
walls to the south of the pier we can see that what survived were
parallel vaults declining in height in a north–south direction (figure
5.3: b and c). The purpose of such a structure within the canon of
first century BCE Roman architectural practice could only be to
support some inclined surface, a ramp or possibly steps, adjacent
to the western wall; a dog-leg type of structural solution becomes
plausible. In 1973, two years after the initial proposition of a stepped
solution to the problem of Robinson's Arch, a further lower vault
of the parallel sequence was excavated to the south of those already
known, with several steps surviving *in situ* on its springing,
confirming beyond doubt the general principle of this interpretation. If we re-read Josephus' text on this area (see above, p. 101),

'and the last led to the other city, where the road descended down into the valley by a great number of steps', it is difficult to see how this reference was ever construed as referring to a bridge. It seems completely consistent with the archaeological findings.

A more precise understanding of the detailing of this monumental public entrance to the Royal Stoa or Basilica of the Temple Mount may never be established for want of further evidence. What is clear, however, is the distinction which the planners of the complex made between public access to the religious and civil functions of the Temple Mount, the Double and Triple Gate passageways and Robinson's Arch steps, rising from opposite ends of the great southern Plaza and concourse area which separates them.

Historical parallels

One of the difficulties which hampered an initial acceptance of a two- or three-sided stepped ramp as a solution to both Robinson's Arch and the eastern arch was the fact that nothing similar was then widely known. Upon further study, however, I found that contemporary parallels are not difficult to establish (figure 5.3: a) both within the Temple Mount area and in the contemporary Roman world. At the southern corner of what is today the women's prayer area of the Western Wall is visible the 2-metre-high lintel of Barclay's Gate, previously mentioned as the third of Josephus' four gates. This Herodian gate leads by a passageway (examined and measured by Warren in the 1860s), to the surface of the Mount from the upper street level parallel to the Western Wall. It follows precisely the same planning concept as that now proposed for Robinson's Arch, a quarter-turn or zig-zag inclined ramp. The only difference is that one is an internal solution while the other is external. The Barclay's Gate passageway is still roofed with a series of parallel, ascending vaults for the lower section, with an inclined vault for the upper, meeting at an half-round cupola with *oculus* at the junction, all of which is presumably supported on arches. A similar vault system may be found in the side chambers of the Temple of Diana at Nimes (first century CE). The arch, vault, dome and relieving arches found here are a comprehensive assembly of Roman constructive forms.

For Robinson's Arch, a more geographically distant contemporary parallel (figure 5.3: a), the first century BCE ampitheatre at Pompeii, has a remarkably similar structure, giving access to the upper tiers of seating from outside. Double arched ramps, with the arches

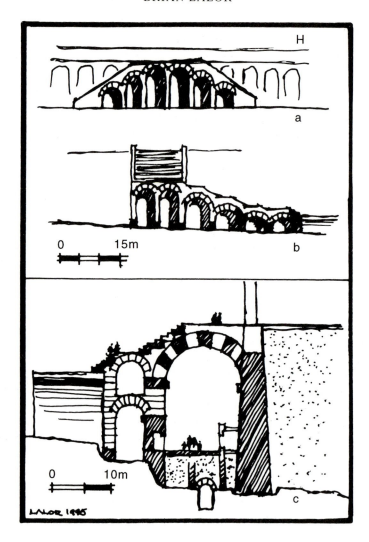

Figure 5.3 Robinson's Arch and Pompeii Amphitheatre compared

Detail 'a' is the still-intact, symmetrical pedestrian access to the Pompeii Amphitheatre, a more elegant and visually satisfactory solution to the same problem.

Detail 'b' looks at the north–south flight of steps of Robinson's Arch, with its graduated declining arches.

Detail 'c' re-assembles the fragments of Robinson's Arch in this east–west cross-section. The vaulted channel beneath the street is the *cloaca maxima* of Herodian Jerusalem.

declining in precisely the same manner as in Jerusalem, indicate the plausibility of this architectural solution. This structural device of the vault is the single unifying constructive principle which underlies the entire project of the Temple Mount platform.

The ascending and descending flights of steps which flank the southern wall (figure 5.2; b) are similarly borne on Pompeii-like sequences of graduated arches, and the Triple Gate undercroft which supports the Temple platform was also supported by monumental parallel vaults.

The accumulated information from the southern area of the Temple Mount, stripped to its structural bones, as revealed by the excavations, argues impressively in favour of a master-hand in the designing of so intensely coherent a solution to the architectural needs of the site and its ecclesiastical/civic functions. The internal logic of the vault is applied rigorously throughout all the areas which are available to excavation or examination; those aspects which appear in some degree of conflict may reflect a paucity of information, more than inconsistency. Any evidence of the use of contemporary techniques of Roman concrete and brick construction is entirely absent from the Temple Mount. It is clear, however, that these methods were practised at the time for private buildings, as is demonstrated in the Herodian palace at Jericho.

This solution to Robinson's Arch also presents a difficulty not easily overcome, although its explanation may lie in an insufficient understanding of the excavated information. This problem concerns the fact that the 15-metre-broad Robinson's Arch has as its continuation a 12.5-metre series of vaults. This makes no sense in planning terms, yet it is difficult to provide an alternative solution. One possibility is the use of the Pompeian model of twin ramps, descending both north and south. More widespread excavation is still required in the area north of the arch to evaluate this proposal. While it might appear to conflict with the excavated evidence, that evidence is too fragmentary to be certain.

THE SOUTH-WEST CORNER

'To the place of trumpeting'

The excavation of the south-western corner of the Temple Mount provided a wealth of archaeological information on certain aspects of its architecture. The area also brought to light one of the single

most important finds relating to the religious rituals of the Temple:
a monumental Hebrew inscription, carved on a fragment of the wall
parapet which lay on the Herodian pavement where the western and
southern streets meet. This metre-high ashlar, with an internal
and external batter, has a niche on its inner face, above which is a
single line of Hebrew characters, *lbythtqy'hlh* (vocalised, 'le bet ha
tkia leha. . .'), which has been interpreted to read 'to the place of
trumpeting, to the . . .'; then the inscription breaks off incomplete.
Josephus is quite specific with regard to the location of this priestly
function. In a passage concerned with John of Gischala's defence of
the Temple Mount during the siege of 70 CE, he wrote:

> The last (tower) was erected over the Temple Chambers, where
> one of the priests stood, and gave a signal beforehand, with a
> trumpet, at the beginning of every seventh day, and in the
> evening twilight, as also in the evening when the day was
> finished, as giving notice to the people when they were to leave
> off work, and when they were to go to work again.
>
> (*Jewish War* IV. ix. 12 [582])

While the 'bet ha tkia' inscription is not the only one to survive
from the Temple platform, this is the only one relating to the religious functions of the Temple which has been found in a
stratigraphically controlled archaeological context. The discovery of
the inscription also casts some light on the destruction of the buildings of the Royal Stoa. As the stone represents the parapet of the
enclosure wall, and was found not among the debris, but sitting on
the street pavement directly below its appropriate position, it can be
deduced that the structure above from which it fell was dismantled
in a methodical manner, course by course, as is described by Josephus.

In first-century BCE Jerusalem, the optimum position, given the
nature of the topography, for a priest to perform the trumpet signal
for the beginning and end of the Sabbath must obviously be a point
of maximum elevation and as close to equidistant from all the quarters of the city as is possible. The south-west corner of the Temple
platform is beyond doubt this position; the parapet of its tower
giving the necessary elevation. The radius, indicated by a dotted line
in the plan, eloquently demonstrates this fact (figure 5.1: B).

The western street

A distinguishing factor about the surface of the great street which
parallels the western wall and its continuation which was excavated

in the Ophel further down the slope in the Tyropoean Valley, by Bliss and Dickie in the 1890s and by Kenyon in the early 1960s, is its pristine condition. It survives in a state quite uncommon to streets from antiquity, looking as though it had been laid not long before the destruction. In structural terms, it is more probable that the great arch spanning the street was constructed before the street, and the evidence of polish on the steps from the arch superstructure, and absence of this on the street certainly suggests installation at a later date. The street, which is stepped in its southmost sections, was apparently for pedestrian use; there is also no evidence of its having been used for vehicular traffic. In *Antiquities*, Josephus relates that building continued under the Roman Procurator Albinus (62–4 CE), and it is possible that part of this street was paved at this time.

Augustan town planning

Perhaps the most remarkable feature of the south-west corner of the Temple precincts (figure 5.4) is the complexity of its circulation problems, and the sophistication of the manner in which these were solved. Large numbers of people were accustomed to visit the city during the three annual pilgrimage festivals, and their comings and goings needed to be manipulated within the constricted space surrounding the Temple. The solution to this problem in this area of the Western Wall was to separate people on a number of different planes, parallel, at right angles to one another and on top of one another. Within the scope of the planning concepts of the period, and in view of the fact that all structures were of heavy ashlar construction, without the use of Roman cement, the results are truly remarkable. The hyperbole of some of Josephus' descriptions, 'these structures seemed incredible to those who had not seen them, and were beheld with amazement by those who had set eyes on them' (*Antiquities* XV. xi. 5 [416]), is less than extravagant when the imaginative excellence of such a small fragment of the overall complex as that of the south-west corner is examined. It is a microcosm of the ambitiousness of Herod's building project and, most enigmatically, it has the imprint of a creative mind, conversant with architecture on the highest plane of conception and development, certainly worthy of the most skilled of Vitruvius' contemporaries.

Of the vast body of (as yet unpublished) architectural, artefactual, numismatic and ceramic evidence which the Temple Mount excavations have revealed, as well as the smaller yet highly significant

Figure 5.4 A view of the western street

body of epigraphic material, the new architectural information must be singled out as contributing more to our understanding of first-century CE Jerusalem than any other single body of finds because it has made available a hitherto unidentified corpus of Herodian structural principles.

The construction of the Temple Mount as we now understand it bears favourable comparison with any contemporary temple precinct of the Roman Empire and deserves to be better appreciated as among the most spectacular building projects of antiquity. In scale it was twice the size of Trajan's Forum, and three times the size of the Sanctuary of Jupiter at Baalbek. Comparisons also may be made in conceptual terms with such sites as the Sanctuary of the Fortuna Primigenia at Palestrina for the manner in which the problems of a complex site are solved, which show Jerusalem as the equal of any such daring undertaking in the Roman world.

Without the literary sources we could not begin to identify the site, and without archaeology we could never attempt to properly understand it. However, the exceptionally valuable information which has been recovered from archaeological excavations since the 1970s, and the corresponding light which this information has cast upon the literary sources, serves to highlight the need for further excavation to resolve the still imperfect state of understanding of many aspects of the Temple Mount. Any future excavations in the area will begin from the position of the advanced understanding which now exists of what constituted the Temple Mount, and from that basis re-examine the still inaccessible question of the Temple and its courts.

CONCLUSION

In conclusion, the everywhere evident technical repertoire of the Temple Mount's designers and builders suggests the strong and direct influence of Roman architectural practice, although the stylistic embellishment of the buildings (entablatures and internal soffit deco-

Figure 5.4 A view of the western street

J A view of the western street which incorporates a cut-away view of Barclay's Gate, and Robinson's Arch seen from the north. The internally vaulted passageway of Barclay's Gate (which has stood for two millennia without collapse) must be supported on some bedrock-based structure. The interpretation shown here assumes that a solution similar to Robinson's Arch most probably lies beneath it. The women's prayer area of the Western Wall is in the immediate foreground

ration, not dealt with here) gives the contrary impresion of more local influence. This dichotomy may be understood as evidence of a master hand in the overall design and engineering concept of Herod's Temple Mount, with local craftsmanship and taste, as well as Jewish strictures against figurative ornament, dictating in the area of the applied arts of sculptural decoration.

The last word deserves to be that of Josephus, dealing in this case with the very mundane question of foundations, which now can be better understood in the light of 'a demonstration on scientific principles'. The concluding sentences of the quotation describe the progress in the construction of the platform, prior to the erection of the superstructure (figure 5.1: K). It reads as a progress report on Herod's building project.

> He also built a wall below, beginning at the bottom, which was encompassed by a deep valley; and at the south side he laid rocks together and bound them to one another with lead, and included some of the inner parts till it proceeded to a great height, and till both the largeness of the square edifice and its altitude were immense, and till the vastness of the stones in the front were plainly visible on the outside, yet so that the inward parts were fastened with iron, and preserved the joints immovable for all future times. When this work (for the foundation) was done in this manner, and joined together as a part of the hill itself to the very top of it, he wrought it all into one outward surface, and filled up the hollow places which were about the wall, and made it a level on the external upper surface, and a smooth level also.
>
> (*Antiquities* XV: xi. 2 [Whiston])

NOTE ON THE FIGURES

All drawings are schematic; the smallness of scale does not allow for dealing with variant interpretations of the materials.

Postscript, April 1996

Recent information regarding the western street indicates that one of my conclusions (the upper level of the street), based on fragmentary evidence, is incorrect, again emphasising the priority of excavation over speculation.

BIBLIOGRAPHY

Avigad, N. (1975) 'The architecture of Jerusalem in the Second Temple period', *Jerusalem Revealed* 41–51, Jerusalem: Israel Exploration Society.

—— (1976) *Archaeological Discoveries in the Jewish Quarter of Jerusalem*, Jerusalem: The Israel Museum (exhibition catalogue).

—— (1980) *Discovering Jerusalem*, Oxford: Basil Blackwell.

Bahat, D. (1980) *Jerusalem, Selected Plans of Historical Sites and Monuments*, Jerusalem: Ariel Publishing House.

Bliss, F. G. and Dickie, A. C. (1898) *Excavations at Jerusalem*, London: Palestine Exploration Fund.

—— (1991) 'The Western Wall tunnels', Jerusalem: *Ariel* 84, 54–84.

—— (1994) 'The Western Wall tunnels', in H. Geva (ed.) *Ancient Jerusalem Revealed*, 170–90, Jerusalem: Israel Exploration Society.

Danby, H. (1933) *The Mishnah*, translated from the Hebrew with an introduction and brief explanatory note, Oxford: Oxford University Press.

Grant, M. (1974) *Cities of Vesuvius*, London: Hamlyn.

Josephus, Flavius *The Jewish War*, trans. G. Williamson (1970), Harmondsworth: Penguin.

—— *The Works of Flavius Josephus*, trans. W. Whiston (n.d.), London: Milner.

Josephus, trans. H. St J. Thackeray and R. Marcus (1956–65), Loeb Classical Library, London: Heinemann; Cambridge, Mass.: Harvard University Press.

Kenyon, K. (1974) *Digging up Jerusalem*, London: Ernest Benn.

Lalor, B. (1969) in B. Mazar 'The excavations in the old city of Jerusalem', *EI* 9 (Hebrew), Jerusalem: Israel Exploration Society.

—— (1969–73) unpublished reconstruction matter: Israel Exploration Society archives.

Mazar, B. (1969) 'The excavations in the old city of Jerusalem', *EI* 9 (Hebrew), Jerusalem: Israel Exploration Society.

—— (1970) 'The excavations south and west of the Temple Mount', Jerusalem: *Ariel* 27, 11–19.

—— (1971) 'The excavations in the old city of Jerusalem near the Temple Mount', *EI* 10 (Hebrew), Jerusalem: Israel Exploration Society.

—— (1974) *Finds from the Archaeological Excavations near the Temple Mount*, Jerusalem: Israel Exploration Society (exhibition catalogue).

—— (1975) *The Mountain of the Lord*, New York: Doubleday.

—— (1975) 'The archaeological excavations near the Temple Mount', *Jerusalem Revealed* 25–40, Jerusalem: Israel Exploration Society.

Netzer, E. (1975) 'The Hasmonean and Herodian winter palaces at Jericho', *IEJ* 25, 89–100.

Robertson, D. S. (1969) *Greek and Roman Architecture*, Cambridge: Cambridge University Press.

Ritmeyer, K. and Ritmeyer, L. (1989), 'Reconstructing Herod's Temple Mount in Jerusalem', *BARev* 15, 23–53.

Ritmeyer, L. (1992) 'Locating the original Temple Mount', *BARev* 18, 24–45.

BRIAN LALOR

Sharon, A., Brutzkus, D. A. and Sharon E. (1973) *Planning Jerusalem:The master plan for the old city of Jerusalem and its environs*, Jerusalem: Weidenfeld and Nicolson.
Vincent, L. H. (1954), *Jerusalem de l'ancien Testament*, Paris: Gabalde.
Vitruvius Pollio, M. *The Ten Books on Architecture*, trans. M. H. Morgan (1960) New York: Dover.
Warren, C. (1869) 'The underground survey of Jerusalem', *ILN*, 24 April.
Warren, C. (1884) *Plans, Elevations, Sections, etc.*, London: Palestine Exploration Fund (portfolio of survey drawings).
Whiston, W. (n.d.) *The Works of Josephus*, London: Milner.
Wilson, C. and Warren, C. (1871) *The Recovery of Jerusalem*, New York: Appleton.

6

ARCHAEOLOGY AND THE HISTORICAL JESUS

Sean V. Freyne

It is sometimes suggested that the current wave of interest in the historical Jesus is due to the recent archaeological findings from Roman Palestine. There is little concrete evidence to support the claim, however, beyond the sometimes over-enthusiastic comparisons made between the Dead Sea Scrolls and Jesus. In this regard little has changed from the origins of the quest for Jesus in the nineteenth century. Browsing today through those lives and their discussion of sources, one is indeed struck by the virtual total silence about aspects of the material culture, apart from the highly romanticised notions of the landscape in Ernest Renan's *La vie de Jésus* (1863). Surveys such as those conducted by Conder and Kitchener (1881), or Guérin (1868–80) came too late, were not known or were considered irrelevant to the tasks of those engaged in the 'first quest' for the historical Jesus. Earlier in this century scholars such as Dalman (1924) and Alt (1949) did focus on aspects of the material culture in dealing with the ministry of Jesus, but their efforts made little or no impression on mainline research about Jesus. Biblical archaeology had already acquired a conservative, apologetic image (which it has not wholly shed even today), and as long as Bultmannian and post-Bultmannian trends dominated 'the new quest' for the historical Jesus it was not likely to receive much of a hearing. Many liberal scholars, operating mainly from the literary sources, still find little of importance to attract them to archaeology, despite the fact that, owing largely to developments in the discipline, we are now in a position to write Renan's 'fifth gospel' in ways and with details that he could never have imagined. Such studies of Jesus as those by Sanders (1984), Crossan (1991), Meier (1991), Chilton (1992) and Borg (1994), to mention some of the more recent, significant offerings, have virtually no mention, and certainly no engagement with the archaeological data dealing with conditions in first-century Palestine that are now available. For other scholars, still under the impression of its apologetic, rather than exploratory nature, mention of archaeology together with Jesus conjures up images of the empty tomb, Peter's house and the Capernaum synagogue, topics best left to pious pilgrims.

This is not the place to discuss the reasons for these biases in contemporary scholarship or to trace the independent growth of various disciplines that should and could have contributed to a joint enterprise. It is encouraging to note signs of change in this regard from both sides of the divide. For some time now archaeologists such as Eric Meyers and James Strange have been insisting on the importance of their findings for the study of early Christianity (Meyers and Strange 1981). New Testament scholars, for their part, are becoming more conscious of the need for dialogue with their 'dirt' colleagues. Thus, during the annual meeting of the Society of Biblical Literature (Chicago 1994) the sections dealing with the archaeology of the New Testament world and the historical Jesus had several joint meetings to which scholars from both sides contributed, marking an important turning-point in the dialogue, even if no firm conclusions were reached (Lull 1994). The large attendance at all the sessions indicates that there is now a growing awareness that the time is ripe for a fruitful dialogue between literary, historical and archaeological approaches to the understanding of the rise and identity of early Christianity.

So what has changed and how do we define the 'new' in both areas? Several developments are worth mentioning briefly. To begin with, biblical archaeology itself has changed considerably in terms of its objectives and method, influenced by developments within the field generally (Scott 1993). These have to do not just with the greater scientific sophistication of pottery analysis, underwater exploration and radar testing for example, but also owe a good deal to the dialogue with the social sciences. As an independent discipline, archaeology is no longer text-driven, as in its earliest phase, but has been developing its own methodology, of which the published report, following area mapping and detailed stratigraphic analysis of sites, has become the standard stock-in-trade. However, an increasing number of studies is concerned with regional and inter-regional comparisons, based on detailed surveying and surface shard-collecting from all existing settlements in a region or sub-region (Dar 1986, 1993; Urman, 1985; Dauphin and Schonfield 1983; Dauphin and Gibson 1993; cf. Barker and Lloyd 1991). In this context increased attention is being given to lesser-known and smaller sites as well as to the larger urban centres. Thus, life in the countryside is gradually being brought into focus as consideration is given to settlements and landscape patterns, the proximity to water and other natural resources, roads, the size of fields and the nature of agricultural cultivation, field towers, wine and olive presses, industrial installations and the like (Applebaum 1986; Fiensey 1991; Frankel 1992; Roll 1983, 1993; Nun 1988; Vitto 1983–4). In order to interpret the mass of data emerging from such surveys, there is, inevitably, an increasing attention to social models that help to map out more comprehensively life as it was lived in pre-industrial societies. In this broader approach archaeology is a natural dialogue partner with ethnography, cultural anthropology and other relevant branches of the social sciences in its efforts to contribute to a more rounded picture of life at various strata of the social spectrum (Meyers and Meyers 1989). It has also meant that archaeology has to correct its positivistic image and self-consciously engage in a hermeneutic enterprise that not only underlines the provisional nature of its findings but also becomes aware of the modern biases that have often determined its findings. In this regard the feminist critique has recently drawn attention to the invisibility of women in many of the current archaeological accounts, thereby challenging modern stereotypes about distinctions that have been drawn between public and private space along gender lines (Sawicki 1995).

At the same time the study of the social world of early Christianity has become increasingly important for many New Testament scholars, especially, but not exclusively, from North America: Studies by Malherbe (1977), Kee (1980) and Meeks (1983) in particular, were trail-blazers following a pioneering article of Smith (1975). Until recently, Theissen (1983) has ploughed a lonely furrow among continental European scholars. In America the Context group, spearheaded by Elliot (1993), Neyrey (1991), Malina and Rohrbaugh (1992) and Esler (1994, 1995), has been most consistent in its application of social theory in explicating various aspects of early Christianity.

Biblical archaeology and New Testament studies, at least that branch that is most concerned with the social world, have, therefore, a common and natural meeting place in the social description of the movement and the circumstances – social, political, economic and religious – that gave rise to this distinctive configuration within the context of Second Temple Judaism. Yet, despite the growing recognition of this on both sides, there is still no consistent method for the wedding of archaeological findings and literary descriptions. Clearly, the old approach, whereby certain pieces of archaeological evidence are introduced to show that the biblical narratives are trustworthy, will not do. Apart from the fact that this approach subordinates archaeology as an independent discipline to the literary evidence, it also smacks of a positivistic outlook that views archaeology as provider of discrete, incontrovertible hard data, that can then be exploited at will by the interpreter of the texts. If archaeology should not be made subservient to the needs of literary historians, neither should it be too dismissive of what have been described as sectarian writings (Vale 1987), giving the impression that archaeologists alone are scientific and objective in their approach, whereas the interpreters of religious texts such as the Gospels may easily fall into the trap of adopting uncritically the partial and therefore biased accounts of the texts with which they deal. An approach that was concerned only with interpreting the remains of material culture is equally open to mistaking the parts for the whole, given the chance nature of many of the most important finds and depending on whether or not the deposition of objects in their present context was accidental or intended. It could equally ignore the fact that those aspects of ancient peoples' lives which gave rise to the sectarian documents may have left very incomplete or indeed no trace at all in the archaeological record.

Each discipline should give its own version of the situation from its perspective, avoiding any easy conflation of these divergent accounts. Rather, they should be juxtaposed and critically evaluated in a two-way dialogue between text and spade (Strange 1992b). Each account challenges the other in various ways, pointing to gaps, possible distortions and emphases that are not likely to have verisimilitude or, alternatively, are capable of illuminating more fully the situation being reconstructed. In such an 'inter-textual' exercise it is important to recognise the methods, shortcomings and assumptions of each discipline, thereby bringing a hermeneutic of suspicion into play. Only after this critical comparison has taken place is it possible to achieve more adequate answers to some pressing questions to do with the historical Jesus and his movement, and the real contribution of archaeology to the debate can be properly evaluated. In the remainder of this paper I want to engage in such an exercise in the hope of developing a more adequate method and of testing its possibilities around specific questions.

THE GEOGRAPHY OF JESUS' MINISTRY

The of crossing boundaries, be they social, political or religious, is usually a way of making a statement, especially if the boundaries are crossed freely. Because of the territorial nature of the Jewish religion which viewed *Eretz Israel* as Yahweh's gift, there was a particular need to pay attention to the precise boundaries of the land, as defined by the religious establishment, irrespective of whether or not these coincided with the political realities of the day. There is later evidence, both literary and inscriptional, to suggest that the rabbis were exercised about the matter, particularly in the north (Sussman 1981). This may have reflected their own concerns after emigrating to Galilee in the wake of the Bar Kochba defeat in the second century. However, the incident reported by Josephus concerning the desire of the Jewish inhabitants of Caesarea-Philippi to purchase oil produced within the land (*Life* 13 [74]) shows that at least some northern Jews were troubled with the issue of purity already in the first century. Thus the movements of Jesus into the non-Jewish areas of Tyre, the Dekapolis and Caesarea-Philippi (Mark 5:1–19; 7:24, 31; 8:27) present an intriguing interpretative problem in regard to his ministry and its primary focus. Should all these travels be viewed as part of a single strategy, as Mark seems to suggest, or could different issues have been at stake in each case?

Various interpreters view the historical significance of these travel notices within the Markan narrative differently. Thus Lang (1978) argues against Dalman (1924) for the historical plausibility of the journey of Mark 7:31, while acknowledging that it now functions within a section of the gospel (Mark 7:24–8; 9) which seeks to anchor the Gentile mission to the actual ministry of Jesus, a position espoused by others also (Marxsen 1956). In a similar vein, Schmeller (1994) has studied thoroughly all these notices from an historical and socio-cultural perspective and concludes that while redactionally they do indeed function as a legitimising of the post-Easter mission, historically they contain a core dealing with the activity of Jesus among Jewish communities within the territories of the Greek cities. After Easter, however, others, non-Jews who also felt alienated in the shadow of the cities and who obtained a new identity in Jesus, were interested in seeing themselves as having been addressed by him also. The story of the Syro-Phoenician woman has attracted the attention of Theissen from the perspective of the local colouring of the narrative. He concludes that because it presupposes an original narrator and audience who are well acquainted with the concrete social and cultural conditions of the region between Tyre and Galilee, it is not so easy to trace the story's origins exclusively to the issue of the legitimacy of the Gentile mission (Theissen 1992: 61–80). He refuses to speculate, however, whether or not the incident belongs to the actual ministry of Jesus.

It would seem then that we are faced with two options for interpreting these geographic notices – *if* in fact they should be seen as referring to the career of Jesus. Either he was engaged in a mission to his co-religionists, and possibly also to other natives, non-Jews who were equally oppressed by urban elites, or he was already concerned with crossing the Jew–Gentile divide, thus opening up the possibility of a Gentile mission before either Paul or the Hellenists. As Sawicki (1995) points out, one crosses boundaries for various reasons – to emigrate, to trade, or to visit. Accordingly, it is important for historians and archaeologists to operate with various models in order to test all the possibilities. Both Schmeller and Theissen are well attuned to the complexity of the literary and archaeological evidence, but the question still needs to be asked whether this necessarily allows for a single interpretation of all the journeys or whether different conditions might not have prevailed in different territories and at different periods. Thus, if Mark's gospel is to be dated close to the Jewish War of 66–70 CE and located somewhere within the region of Syria–Palestine, as an increasing number of interpreters seem to agree, then one would have to ask whether or not the tensions between Jew and Greek in the north that Josephus describes (*Jewish War* II. xviii.1, 2 [457–65]; cf. *Life* 23 [113]) might have had a bearing on the ethnocentric references both in the Syro-Phoenician story and in the earlier one dealing with the Gadarene demoniac (Freyne 1994: 82–4). Can an independent canvassing of the archaeological evidence help, while being true to the methods of the discipline?

With regard to immigration, archaeology can provide some important perspectives. In 1976, the Meiron excavation project headed by Eric Meyers, James Strange and Denis Groh conducted a survey of a total of nineteen sites in Upper and Lower Galilee and just two in the Golan, at locations where the remains of ancient synagogues were known. They concluded that a cultural continuum existed between Upper Galilee and the Golan on the basis of obvious similarities of architectural styles for synagogues, the absence of representational art and the predominance of Hebrew–Aramaic inscriptions as well as common pottery types. This pattern was not in their opinion maintained in Lower Galilee where different influences could be detected (Meyers *et al.* 1978; Meyers 1976, 1985). While some of their conclusions have had to be modified in the light of subsequent findings, the cultural relationship between Upper Galilee and the Golan has been reinforced by a more detailed survey in the Golan by Urman (1985). According to his findings the number of settlements in the Golan increased from seventy-five in the Hellenistic to 182 in the Roman period. There are variations in different sub-regions and Urman does not distinguish between the Early, Middle and Late Roman periods. Nevertheless, when all the factors are taken into account, especially the strong Jewish presence there of later times, the steady increase points strongly in the direction of internal migration from the Early Roman period onwards, probably already following the Hasmonean annexation of the north. The region in question within the Golan could easily be covered by the rather curious Markan phrase 'in the midst of the Dekapolis', once it is recalled that according to Pliny, Damascus to the north-east was one of the ten cities of this region, even though the others are clustered much further to the south (Lang 1978: 147–52). In that event Jesus' journey would have been to a thoroughly Jewish territory, a fact that Josephus also seems to take for granted more than once by saying in one place that Judas the Galilean, the founder of the Fourth Philosophy, was a native of Gamala in the Golan (*Antiquities* XVIII. i.1 [4]), and by describing his own appointment as governor by the revolutionary council in 66 CE to the two Galilees *and Gamala* (*Jewish War* II. xx. 4 [566–8).

The situation with regard to the territory of Tyre and Sidon and Caesarea-Philippi is rather different, at least from an archaeological profile. No remains of a Jewish presence such as synagogues or *miqva'oth*, have been found above a line that runs from Sasa through Baram to Qatzyon (Ilan 1986–7). In the west, similarly, a clear demarcation can be drawn between places yielding evidence of Jewish culture in the material remains and those that do not (Aviam 1993), and this would presumably correspond with ancient territorial boundaries. This does not mean, of course, that no Jews lived outside those lines. The later rabbinical concerns suggest that such was not the case, and there are indications from Josephus, as we have seen, that Jews lived in both Caesarea-Philippi and Tyre. It must, however, signify a very different ethos, even for Jews living in country places, than that which would have obtained for their counterparts in the

Golan. Were Jesus to have visited these latter, one could conceive the purpose and function of the visit in rather different terms from a visit to Jewish communities in the Golan, therefore.

This raises the second reason for boundary crossing, namely, trading purposes. Links between Tyre and Galilee in this regard go back to the time of Solomon, and were also emphasised by Ezekiel in the sixth century BCE (1 Kgs 5:11; 17:7–16; Ezek 27:17). Because of its location on an island with a very narrow strip of land between it and the mountainous, mainland promontory, Tyre, despite its wealth from seafaring, was, nevertheless, dependent on its hinterland for its basic sustenance (Acts 12:20). As a recognised port it would also have functioned as a collecting and export centre for any surplus goods such as grain and oil. It comes as no surprise, therefore, to find that Tyrian coins predominate at the Jewish sites in Upper Galilee excavated by the Meiron expedition (Hanson 1980; Raynor and Meshorer 1988). What is more surprising is that the same holds for Lower Galilee also (Barag 1982–3), though we must await the publication of the numismatic evidence from the various digs currently in progress, especially at Sepphoris, before coming to any definitive conclusions for this region.

A number of reasons can be suggested for this situation. In all probability Tyre, because of its traditional status, was allowed by Rome to mint a far greater number of coins than was permissible at such local mints as Sepphoris and Tiberias, or even Acco-Ptolemais. This could mean that, as Horsley (1994: 105f.) claims, too much should not be read into the frequency of these coins in Galilee in terms of trading links with Tyre. It is true that, unlike pottery remains which we shall presently discuss, coin finds can only tell us about their place of origin and final deposition, but nothing about their intermediate use for trading or other purposes. Horsley's critique of Meyers and Hanson is too dismissive of the literary evidence for such links, however. Neither does it do justice to the fact that in all the hoards of coins found in the north (Magdala, Gischala and especially Isfija, Carmel) city coins from Tyre predominate. This latter hoard of some 5,000 Tyrian tetradrachmas and didrachmas contained coins dated to the few years before Nero put an end to their production, replacing them instead with provincial coins of lesser silver content and weight. In the absence of a resident Roman army in Palestine in the first century, for the payment of which most of the coins struck in antiquity were required (Duncan-Jones 1994), the existence of such a large hoard suggests serious trading links with Tyre, unless one were to posit their collection for religious purposes only. Even then, however, the money would have had to have been obtained on some basis. Because of its stable value, compared with other currencies, the Tyrian didrachma continued to be 'the coin of the sanctuary' according to rabbinical ruling (*Mishnah, Bek.* 8: 7; *Tosefta Ketubot* 13: 3; see Danby 1933) and they remained in circulation for well over a hundred years after their last striking. Thus, as well as the secular economy, the Temple economy meant that there was a demand for Tyrian money in Palestine throughout the first century (Ben-David 1969). This was all the more surprising in view of the pagan religious symbolism of the coins associated with the city, and can only be attributed to the buying power and consistency of the money, thereby underlining the continued importance of the city for the economy of the hinterland, both religious and everyday.

If, then, the case for trading links between Tyre and Galilee can still in general be maintained, it does not yet explain why a Galilean teacher-prophet might want to visit the region of the city, especially in view of Jesus' critique of wealth and possessions. One could argue, as does Schmeller (1994: 49f.), that Jews living in the countryside of these city territories were just as likely to be exploited as were their non-Jewish peasant neighbours, given the way in which the economy in agrarian societies was controlled politically (Oakman 1994: 229f.; Freyne 1995b). Schmeller bases his conclusion on the fact that within Galilee itself, Jesus' ministry seems to have been conducted in the villages of Lower Galilee for the most part, a subregion where, according to the Meiron survey (1978), the influences of Hellenistic culture were being felt. He interprets this to mean that the traditional way of life was coming under threat from the effects of urbanisation in the region. We shall discuss this issue in detail in the next section. Here it is of importance in suggesting a possible socio-economic reason for Jesus' visit to the region of Tyre as well as to the villages of Caesarea-Philippi. The force of the suggestion stems from the fact that it plausibly links the ministry of Jesus in these places with that in Galilee itself. On the other hand the visit to the Dekapolis region could not be so easily explained on the same basis, provided our suggestion of the Jewish ethos of such a visit has any merit.

At this juncture recent discussion of the pottery trade opens up interesting possibilities for understanding such forays beyond the Jordan. The focus has been on the ceramic industry at two Galilean villages, both of which were known from rabbinical literature for the quality of their pottery – Kefr Hanania, located between Upper and Lower Galilee, and Shikhin, near Sepphoris. Detailed neutron activation analysis (NAA) of the provenance and distribution of the Kefr Hanania household ware by David Adan-Bayewitz (1993) points in his view to a network of trading links between this Galilean village, not just with other centres within Galilee itself, notably Sepphoris (Adan-Bayewitz and Perlman 1990), but with both Jewish and non-Jewish settlements in the Golan also. In competition with local ware there, Kefr Hanania is estimated to have provided 10–20 per cent of the total needs. The distribution pattern shows that the closer any given location was to the production centre, the greater the total percentage of wares from that centre was. Nevertheless, products from Kefr Hanania were also found at Acco-Ptolemais and Caesarea (Banias), but significantly not south of the Nazareth ridge nor in the urban centres of Scythopolis and Samaria, thus confirming local separatism based on religious animosities (cf. Lk 9:53; Jn 4:9). Shikhin seems to have specialised in stone jars and supplied not just Sepphoris, but other centres also, possibly even Cana (Strange, Groh and Longstaff 1994).

In view of the fact that the wares from both centres are singled out for special mention in the Rabbinic literature, one could argue with some justification that the appearance of Kefr Hanania ware at centres outside Galilee, even non-Jewish ones, is best explained by halachic concerns of some of the inhabitants of these places, by analogy with the Jews of Caesarea-Philippi, who, according to Josephus, were prepared to pay extra to obtain oil from the land because of similar concerns (*Life* 13 [74f.]; cf. *Jewish War* II. xxi. 2 [591–3]). This is not the conclusion that Adan-Bayewitz draws from his study, however. The absence of the competing Golan ware at any of the Galilean sites calls for some explanation, especially if one is to talk about trading networks and Galilean culture being open to outside influences and posit the existence of extensive trading links, as others drawing on his conclusions have done. In this regard it is important to avoid modern ideas about both manufacture and market, given the nature and scale of the operations which were very much rooted in local needs, and were small-scale and family-based in terms of production and distribution (Vitto 1983–4; McMullen 1970).

It is clear from this discussion that archaeology cannot settle the question of either the fact or the function of Jesus' visits to the surrounding territories. What it can do is to help a better under-standing of the day-to-day contacts that did exist in that region, and provide us with a number of alternatives for judging both the verisimilitude and possible intention of any such visits against that background. In the end one's understanding of any given episode and its likely impact will depend on the assumptions one brings to the discussion of what Jesus' overall intentions might have been. Schmeller's suggestion that a ministry to Jews living in these outlying areas because of the pressures they were experiencing in economic rather than cultural terms is attractive in that it does point to a deliberate pattern which, we shall presently see, appears to be consis-tent with Jesus' strategy in Galilee also, namely that of avoiding the urban centres. There must surely be something significant in Mark's careful portrayal of his visiting the *land* of the Gadarenes, the *borders* of Tyre and the *villages* of Caesarea-Philippi, but not the actual urban centres. But what are the reasons for such a strategy? All one can say for definite is that on the basis of our present knowledge of Jewish settlement patterns in the area in the first century, such journeys and contacts would be consistent with somebody who was not only concerned with socio-economic oppression of co-religionists and the consequent erosion of kinship values, but who also believed himself to have a ministry to call all Israel to a new vision of its own destiny. Indeed, both concerns would have been mutually reinforcing.

JESUS AND THE HERODIAN CULTURE OF GALILEE

Apart from Luke's account, the virtual absence of Herod Antipas and his court from the story of Jesus is remarkable, particularly in view of the close association with the Baptist, whom Herod perceived to be a political threat (Josephus: *Antiquities* XVIII. v. 2 [119–19]). The silence becomes even more striking when one considers that, during the life-time of Jesus, Antipas had refurbished Sepphoris and had founded Tiberias, probably in the year 19 CE, thereby seeking to emulate the building feats of his father, Herod the Great – on a more modest scale to be sure. Both foundations were undoubtedly intended to honour his imperial patron, possibly in the hope of eventually becoming king of the Jews, instead of mere tetrarch.

The silence of the gospels concerning these urban centres of Lower Galilee should have raised questions for historical Jesus researchers, one would have thought. Yet, with one or two exceptions this does not seem to have occurred. Already in 1926 Shirley Jackson Case discussed the issue of Jesus and Sepphoris, attempting to explain some of Jesus' attitudes – his pacifism and his openness to strangers – on the basis of his having grown up close to Sepphoris and possibly having worked there as a *tekton*. As yet no serious archaeological work had been done at the site, but more recently, Richard Batey has attempted to revive Case's approach, drawing on his experience as part of the University of South Florida Sepphoris Project under the direction of James Strange. He attributes, among other things, Jesus' friendship with tax-collectors to his experience of the pro-Roman, anti-Zealot stance of the people of Sepphoris in the first century (Batey 1984a, 1984b, 1991).

While Case and Batey attempt to explain certain aspects of Jesus' ministry, including some of the attributed sayings, to his contact with the urban environment of Sepphoris, Albrecht Alt adopted the opposite position. He argued for Nazareth's isolation from the capital on the basis of rather dubious geophysical grounds. According to him 'a wall of separation' existed between the two places, with Nazareth oriented more to the great plain in the south, and Sepphoris inclined towards the plain of Acco (Alt 1949).

These attempts to discuss the issue of Jesus and Sepphoris must be deemed unsatisfactory, because the question is being addressed from a far too narrow focus, giving rise to highly speculative arguments from silence that are ultimately unconvincing. Recent developments in socio-archaeology, already mentioned, are concerned with discerning the pattern of relationships between town and country (Rich and Wallace-Hadrill 1991), and offer a more realistic possibility for addressing the question in a meaningful way. The contribution of James Strange is particularly noteworthy, in so far as he deals directly with the matter for Sepphoris and its environs (Strange 1992a). He speaks of an urban overlay which in his view indicates close bonds between the city and the countryside, the city being dependent on its hinterland for such natural resources as its water supply, while at the same time providing an outlet for goods produced by the peasants, whether agricultural produce (grain, oil and wine) or pottery and stone jars from Kefr Hanania and Shikhin, as previously discussed. The large underground silos for storage in Sepphoris as well as the discovery of a lead weight inscribed on both sides in Greek, *agoranomoi* ('market inspectors'), point to the city as having both a market and an administrative role in Lower Galilee

(Meyers 1986). Josephus is also aware of this dual role, on the one hand chiding Sepphoris for not resisting the Romans even though it was well supplied by surrounding villages (*Life* 65 [346]), and on the other mentioning the jealousy of Justus of Tiberias because his native place had to cede to it both the banking and the records (*archaiai*) under Nero (*Life* 9 [38]).

In arguing for a symbiotic relationship between Sepphoris and its hinterland, Strange is challenging the dominant view, associated in particular with Moses Finley, that ancient cities were parasitic on the countryside (Finley 1977). Others too have questioned this view, arguing that from the Hellenistic age onwards, cities engaged in production and increased marketing, and so were able to pay the peasants for their produce, thus enabling these to pay their taxes in money rather than in kind (Hopkins 1980; Wallace-Hadrill 1991). There appear to be some grounds for modifying somewhat Finley's views, but without blurring the undoubted distinctions between city and country in antiquity, something that can be easily documented from both literary and archaeological sources (Whittaker 1991). Urbanisation and urban overlay could easily become terms for a one-way process that does not do justice to the complex relationship that undoubtedly existed. It may well be the case that, strictly on the basis of the data drawn from the material remains, this is in fact the picture that suggests itself to field archaeologists in view of the formal continuities between urban and smaller settlements. They must recognise, however, that when it comes to interpreting those same data within a more general theory of social relations in antiquity, they require theoretical models appropriate to the task they set themselves (Carney 1975; Elliot 1993).

Strange assumes that the encounter with Hellenism had prepared the Galileans for Antipas' aggressive Romanisation, thus enabling the locals to make a powerful symbolic statement in stone of how they viewed the world, grafting together the native and the imported without any real confrontation between them. This can be seen from the material remains of Jewish Sepphoris where the process has, in his view, reached down to the very lowest levels of city life, and extended itself to the surrounding region as well. Even the words of Jesus reflect the process, echoing as many urban as rural images and types (Strange 1992a, 1992b).

This view of the matter assumes that the 'urban overlay' which Strange detects in the material culture of Lower Galilee was perceived in the same light by all the inhabitants of the region. The question has to be asked whether all might have benefited equally from the contacts. Was the symbolic statement celebrating the power of Rome which Sepphoris and Tiberias were intended to make perceived in the same way at all levels of the social spectrum even among the urban inhabitants? Given the fact that no individual or sub-group ever fully internalises a culture in all its aspects, can one confidently assume that the Galilean peasants, even those tied to Sepphoris by economic or other reasons, were equally impressed by all aspects of the dominant culture represented by the city? To be sure, Sepphoris differed in this regard from such centres as Beth Shean-Scythopolis and Akko-Ptolemais, where even from the Early Hellenistic Age both literary and archaeological evidence point to aggressive Hellenisation. Yet, despite the more modest signs of Romanisation that the Herodian centres represented, it is difficult to explain Galilee's participation in the revolt of 66 CE if they had been as successful in creating a single symbolic world as Strange's analysis would seem to suggest. There are many ways of resisting imperialist ideology, even when the external trappings of colonial power, including language, have to be adopted for commercial or adminis-trative reasons.

My query to those who espouse the urbanisation hypothesis, there-fore, is not about the urban overlay that may be detected in the material culture, but rather about the ways in which people felt free to resist, dissent, select or develop counter-cultural models to the prevailing ones. It is doubtful if archaeology can assist us directly in answering this question. As Strange recognises, apart from the Jerusalem temple, the synagogue is the most typically Jewish building where a different cultural experience could be fostered. Closely allied to this are the *miqva'oth* or ritual baths where the separation that the purity laws embodied was ritually expressed on a regular basis. The pre-70 CE archaeological evidence for both structures is sparse, though existing at Gamala (both synagogue and *miqveh*), Khirbet Shema and Sepphoris (*miqva'oth*) and Magdala (presumed syna-gogue), Jotapata (reported *miqveh*). This scarcity so far of evidence for the instrumentalities of the Jewish way of life from the pre-70 CE period is all the more surprising in view of the fact that the Gospels, and to a lesser extent Josephus, seem to assume the pres-ence of synagogues throughout the region (Mark 1:39; Mt 4:23; Lk 4:15; *Life* 54 [277]), causing some to challenge its Jewish char-acter, in favour of either a Hellenised or an Israelite alternative. On the other hand Zvi Ma'oz has proposed the novel theory that, since the building of synagogues was a political act in Roman Palestine as elsewhere, they were allowed from the time of Herod onwards only at the larger urban centres and the district capitals, but not in the villages. It was only in the third century and afterwards, when Jewish resistance as a political threat had been broken, that synagogue building occurred on the grand scale, even in remote areas. Even then, however, it was not without political significance that a Greco-Roman urban architectural type was defiantly transferred and adapted to lesser Jewish settlements. Prior to that, Jewish communities in more remote settlements gathered in less formal contexts such as courtyards or private dwellings, or even in the open air (Ma'oz 1992).

This situation inevitably recalls the strategy of Jesus, at least as it is represented in the Gospels. His ministry avoided the urban centres, not just in the surrounding territories, as we have seen, but even in the heartland of Galilee itself. He concentrated instead on the villages, where the worst aspects of the pressure downwards from the top of the social pyramid were most keenly felt. In terms of the kingdom of God which he proclaimed, it was the *ptochoi* that he declared blessed. These are not the same as the *penes* or the poor. Rather they are those who have lost their status or had it removed from them through loss of property (Malina and Rohrbaugh 1992: 48f.). At the same time he castigated the rich and called on them to share their goods with the needy, thereby radically challenging the social norms of honour, power and patronage as these operated at centres such as Sepphoris. Elsewhere, I have attempted to show that Jesus' critique of secular kingship, in one instance in the context of declaring the imminent downfall of Beelzebul's kingdom, is best understood as a covert critique of Herodian kingship rather than a generalised set of remarks (Freyne 1995a). But what was the inspiration for this movement of protest and what was the shared understanding of prophet and addressees? Those who see the region as a whole as highly urbanised and Hellenised assume a total openness of the inhabitants to the religio-philosophical ideas emanating from the cities, particularly Cynicism, the popular counter-cultural philosophy of Greco-Roman society (Mack 1988, 1993; Downing 1992; Crossan 1991). The support for this position is sought in the archaeological record as propounded by Overman (1988, 1993) and Edwards (1988, 1992), both of whom follow Strange's position broadly speaking. This provides Crossan with the perfect setting for his a priori unlikely construct of a peasant Jewish Cynic. Yet perhaps

SEAN V. FREYNE

archaeology has something more to say on this topic, namely the provenance and religious affiliations of Galileans. It is to this crucial issue in historical Jesus research that we must now finally turn.

A JEWISH GALILEE?

The issue of the religious and cultural affiliations of the Galilean population in the first century is central to historical Jesus research because of its theological, as well as its historical implications, even today. H. D. Betz has recently shown that those who currently espouse a Cynic Jesus are, unwittingly or otherwise, successors of those who in the last century sought to revive Cynicism as a world philosophy, particularly under the patronage of Friedrich Nietzsche. As a forerunner to his *Welt-Philosophie* he, too, considered a Jesus who had left behind the narrow confines of Judaism and had not yet been Christianised (Betz 1994). In a similar vein the notion of a cosmopolitan Galilee, open to and receptive of all the cultural influences of the Greco-Roman society, also has a nineteenth-century forerunner from the History of Religions School in the work of Schürer (1886), Bauer (1927) and Bertram (1935). The result, if not the intention, was to detach Jesus from his Jewish roots, a conclusion that reached its explicit formulation in the 1941 declaration of Grundman that Jesus 'kein Jude war'. This anti-Jewish bias in much of nineteenth-century scholarship, already blatantly expressed in Renan's contrasting depictions of the Galilean and Judean landscapes and the different religious orientations in terms of gospel and law emanating from each (1863), has been exposed in recent times (Klein 1978). It would be a false ecumenism in a post-Holocaust era to attempt to gloss over the tensions between the nascent Jesus movement and its Jewish matrix. At the same time it is equally incumbent on scholars to consider all the implications of their scholarly reconstructions and to examine as dispassionately as possible all the available evidence.

Archaeology can assist by giving its own independent account of the data that would point to the ethnic mix within the population of first-century Galilee. While general adaptation to the environment of a particular place is common to all people, irrespective of their ethno-religious affiliations, certain features of lifestyles may be discernible in such material remains as public buildings, baths, coins, etc. that can point strongly in one direction or another. In the case of first-century Galilee three different proposals can be detected in recent and contemporary discussions: the Galileans were the remnants of an old Israelite population (Alt); there was an enforced Judaicisation by the Hasmoneans of the Iturean people who had infiltrated most of Galilee (Schürer 1886: 7–10); or a colonisation from the south following the Hasmonean conquest of the north in the late second and early first century BCE. While none of these suggestions necessarily excludes one or both of the others, it would seem legitimate to draw certain wider inferences on the basis of which background was likely to have been the more dominant among the first-century population of Galilee. A process of inculturation over a few generations can begin to blur, at least at the level of everyday interaction, any distinctions that large-scale population disruptions may have initially given rise to. Yet, group traits are also shaped by tradition and memory, especially if imposed colonisation has brought about the disruptions in the first instance. With these *caveats* in mind, the question to be addressed has to do with how archaeology might assist in determining the religious loyalties in the first century of those whom our literary sources call 'Galileans'.

The findings of Zvi Gal's survey (mid-1970s; Gal 1992) of Iron Age III sites (i.e. seventh–sixth century BCE) challenge Alt's contention, argued from the literary sources for the most part, that the Israelite population in the Galilee was relatively undisturbed throughout centuries, thus providing the framework for the incorporation of the region into the *ethnos ton Ioudaion* by the Hasmoneans in the second century BCE (Alt 1953–64). Alt believed that Galilee had fared better in the first Assyrian onslaught of 732 BCE than Samaria did in 721 BCE, when the native population was replaced by people of non-Israelite stock (2 Kgs 15:29; 17:6, 24). The absence from eighty-three surveyed sites in Lower Galilee of four different pottery types, dated to that particular period on the basis of stratified digs at Hazor and Samaria, has convinced Gal that there was a major depopulation of the area in the century after the fall of Samaria. Only additional stratified digs will decide whether this population gap was the result of the Assyrian aggression or was due to the migration of the country people to larger settlements. In any event, the theory that the rural population of Galilee remained untouched by the Assyrian invasion would seem to be challenged by such findings.

What can archaeology say about the Iturean hypothesis? Josephus reports (*Antiquities* XIII. xi. 3 [318–19]) on the enforced Judaization by Judah Aristobulus I in 105 BCE of the Itureans, a semi-nomadic

Arab people who became sedentarised in the Hellenistic period and who are associated particularly with the Hermon region (Dar 1993). The claim is that with the break-up of the Seleucid empire during the second century BCE, the Itureans infiltrated Upper Galilee – according to some (Schürer 1979: 7–10, for example), almost all of Galilee – which, it is suggested, was hitherto sparsely populated. Recent archaeological evidence would seem to pose a number of difficulties for this scenario, however. First, Upper Galilee was not so sparsely populated in the Early Hellenistic period, as the results of the archaeological survey already alluded to make clear (Aviam 1993). Nor is the character of the settlements similar to those confidently identified as Iturean in the Golan (Kh. Zemel, e.g., Hartel 1987), since the Upper Galilean settlements reflect a sedentarised and agricultural rather than a semi-nomadic, pastoral milieu, so obvious in the Golan remains, at least for the initial phase of sedentarisation there in the Persian period. The majority of these Iturean sites are in eastern (i.e. Upper) Golan, but there are signs of expansion to the south-west in the direction of Galilee (Hartel 1985–6). According to Aviam (1993), many settlements in Upper Galilee were abandoned in the Hellenistic period, only to have been replaced by others which from the preponderance of Hasmonean coins he regards as Jewish, probably from the period of the expansion in the second century BCE. There may well have been Iturean settlements also, since, to complicate the matter further, shards have been found in Upper Galilee which, in terms of clay composition (pinkish brown with coarse grits) and style (from large storage jars, poorly finished), are not dissimilar to so-called 'Iturean ware' from Hermon-Golan (Epstein and Gutmann 1972; Urman 1985: 162–4; Hartel 1989: 124–6).

The current political situation has prevented further surveying of the western Hermon region (modern southern Lebanon), which might reveal a greater Iturean presence than can be postulated at present. Irrespective of what might be the final judgement on that issue, the notion of Iturean conversions accounting for most of the Jews of the Galilee comes from an uncritical reading of Josephus, who is reporting Strabo's citation of Timagenes, which is taken to parallel a similar description (*Antiquities* XIII. ix. 1 [257–8]) of the treatment of the Idumeans in the south by the Hasmoneans (Kasher 1988). It is noteworthy, however, that unlike Idumeans such as Herod, no Galilean is ever described as a half-Jew in the rabbinic literature, despite the suspicion of Galileans as *'am ha-'aretz* by the standards of the sages (Oppenheimer 1977). Thus, neither literary nor archaeological evidence supports the hypothesis, but indicates rather that if there were Itureans in Upper Galilee in the Early Hellenistic period, they left with the advance of the Hasmonean armies of conquest, an option which they were given according to Josephus (*Antiquities* XIII. xi. 3 [318]).

It was only in the Persian and Early Hellenistic periods that signs of new settlements began to appear in this area once more. Preliminary results from the Archaeological Survey of Israel for Upper Galilee show an upward curve from ninety-three sites in the Hellenistic period to 138 for the Roman and 162 for the Byzantine periods respectively (Aviam 1993). As already noted, this trend corresponds to the results of Urman's survey of the Golan carried out for the Association for the Archaeological Survey of Israel and the Israel Antiquities Authority (1985). It is best explained in terms of the incorporation of the whole Galilee–Golan region into the Jewish state and the need for new settlements and military outposts on both sides of the Jordan. The further increase of settlements in the Roman and Byzantine periods is directly attributable to internal Jewish migration for the most part, both in the wake of the second revolt and as a result of the increased Christian presence in the south from the fourth century CE onwards.

The task of identifying sites as Jewish or not is a difficult one, since, as already noted, such instrumentalities of Jewish life as synagogues and *miqva'oth* are scarce for the pre-70 period. The presumption, nevertheless, is that sites which can be clearly identified as Jewish on the basis of the synagogue remains, with their distinctively Jewish iconography, inscriptions, and liturgical architecture, especially in Upper Galilee–Golan from the Middle Roman to the Early Arab period, in all probability were not all new foundations, but were based in some instances at least on existing Jewish settlements from the earlier period. Stratified digs have been able to confirm this assumption at such sites as Meiron, Khirbet Shema, Gush ha-Lab in Upper Galilee. Architectural remains of synagogues from Lower Galilee are less well preserved, with a few notable exceptions (Khorazin, Capernaum, Hammath Tiberias). Nonetheless, a recent survey of some seventy sites shows almost as many remains for Lower as for Upper Galilee (Ilan 1986–7). This evidence would seem to support the third possibility suggested, namely, Hasmonean colonisation from the south as the most likely hypothesis for explaining the dominant Jewish element in first-century Galilee presumed by the literary sources. It is the preponderance of Hasmonean coins at bedrock in several of these sites that has convinced Aviam that these were in fact Jewish sites, especially in view of the propaganda nature of those early Jewish coins. Such an hypothesis would best explain the continued resistance to Herod the Great in Galilee because of his ousting of the Galilean nobles which Jospehus reports, and it would also account for the on-going Jerusalem–Galilee relations which both Josephus and the Gospels assume (Freyne 1987, 1988b). The absence of any human or animal representations on the coins of Herod Antipas, the first to be struck in Galilee itself, would appear to support such a general conclusion, particularly when compared with those of his brother Philip in the neighbouring kingdom. The coin of the First Revolt from Gamala with the inscription, 'For the Redemption of Jerusalem, the Holy' (Gutman and Wagner 1986–7) together with the *miqva'oth* already mentioned, point to some concern with purity and holiness as represented by the Jerusalem Temple in the archaeological remains also.

This does not mean that non-Jews, or Jews of another provenance, possibly even those of old Israelite stock, did not also make up part of the population mix. Josephus tells of the distinctively Jewish way of life that the Babylonian Jews whom Herod the Great had planted in Gaulanitis and Trachonitis were able to maintain (*Antiquities* XVII. ii. 1–3 [23–31]). In addition there is evidence that Dan continued as a cult-centre in the Hellenistic Age on the basis of the bi-lingual (Aramaic and Greek) dedicatory inscription 'to the God who is in Dan' (Biran 1981; Tzaferis 1992b). Only a narrow view of observant Jewish practice and its inability to live in mixed communities requires an ethnically cleansed Galilee. What emerges from the map of known Jewish settlements, especially where synagogue remains have been claimed, is a concentration of sites in certain areas of both Galilees. In those districts there are few, if any remains of a non-Jewish presence, whereas outside those sub-regions the evidence is unmistakable. The situation is most obvious in Upper Galilee, where a Roman temple from the second century CE at Qedesh points to a thriving pagan culture (Aviam 1985; Fischer *et al.* 1984, 1986). Farther north the bi-lingual inscription from Dan, as well as the grotto of Pan at Banias dating from Seleucid times at least (Tzaferis 1992a), show that the region south of Hermon was thoroughly hellenised from an early period (Biran 1981; Tzaferis 1992b). Herod the Great dedicated a temple to Augustus at Caesarea Philippi (*Jewish War* I. xxi. 3 [404–6]; *Antiquities* XV. x. 3 [363–4]). As mentioned previously, no material remains of Jewish presence have been found above a line that runs just north of Sasa, Baram and Qazyon, all of which show unmistakable signs of having been Jewish communities. To the west–south–west no synagogal remains have been found west of the line Peqi'in to Rama in Upper Galilee, and a similar situation obtains in Lower Galilee west of the line running from Rama through I'billin to Tiv'on (Ilan 1986–7; Aviam 1993). In the south no clear evidence of Jewish communities has been found south of the Nazareth ridge. Outside these lines one is moving in the orbit of the Greek cities, especially Beth-Shean-Scythopolis and Acco-Ptolemios, while to the north Tyre was the dominant urban influence, even on Jewish Galilee, as we have seen.

As well as the absence of synagogues or other material signs of Jewish presence in these areas, dedicatory inscriptions to pagan gods have so far been found only on the fringes of Galilee, such as the third-century CE inscription addressed in Greek to the Syrian gods, Hadad and Atargatis from the region of Acco-Ptolemais, or the one addressed to the Heliopolitan Zeus on Mount Carmel. (Avi-Yonah 1951, 1959). On the other hand, the only remains of pagan worship from Jewish Galilee (apart from some personal votive objects from Sepphoris) is the Syro-Egyptian shrine at Har Mispe Yamim in the Meiron massif, a site which was abandoned already in the second century BCE (Frankel 1989–90). The Jewish and non-Jewish areas were not hermetically sealed from one another, however. The evidence points only to the predominant ethnic identities being localised. The literary evidence that there were Jews living in the city territories of Palestine and that some non-Jews were also to be found in Jewish areas, is not negated. In both instances they would have constituted minorities that were more or less influential on their immediate environment at different periods.

This distinction between Jewish and non-Jewish elements in Galilee is strikingly confirmed by Christian remains. Early archaeological work concentrated on the important Christian sites associated with the life of Jesus, such as Nazareth, Mount Tabor, Capernaum and Tabhga. In these areas it would seem that Jews and Christians lived side by side from the Middle Roman period (i.e. second century CE onwards) until the Persian conquest in 614 CE (Bagatti 1971). A similar pattern emerges for the Golan also (Dauphin and Schonfield 1983; Dauphin and Gibson 1992–3). In western Galilee, however, Aviam (1993) has found many Christian settlements, identified by the number of crosses as well as dedicatory inscriptions on remains of tombs and churches. Some of the inscriptions are in Syriac and others are in Greek, suggesting that some of the local semitic, non-Jewish population may have converted to Christianity. This concentration of a Christian presence in western Galilee seems to corroborate the fact that in that area at least, bordering on the territories of the Phoenician cities, the non-Jewish element continued to predominate from pre-Christian to Christian times.

CONCLUSION

This examination of archaeology's contribution to our understanding of the population patterns of Galilee in the first century CE appears to challenge the picture of a predominantly non-Jewish region, or at least one that was thoroughly open to all and every cultural influence coming from the larger Greco-Roman society. The kind of cultural ambience that is required to support the Cynic hypothesis, at least in the rural areas, would appear to be missing. The conclusion does not of itself disprove the hypothesis, but simply points to the fact that the population of Galilee, Upper and Lower, in the first century CE contained a sufficient number of people whose cultural and religious roots were linked with the south, thereby identifying with Jerusalem and its Temple. This suggestion corresponds with what the literary sources in their very different ways also portray. The extent to which Jesus was inspired by such links cannot be determined from archaeology. Only detailed comparison of the ethos of his sayings, critically examined, with both their Jewish and non-Jewish parallels, can decide how far his world-view was shaped by the Jewish religious experience or by that of popular Greco-Roman philosophy. What this study has hopefully shown is that those who seek to support their picture of Cynic influences on Jesus and his audience cannot do so unambiguously on the basis of the archaeological evidence. It has also sought to demonstrate that by allowing archaeology its own voice, it can act as a challenge and a corrective to our texts, ancient and modern, while acknowledging the provisional nature of its own conclusions. Only an on-going critical dialogue in which both disciplines operate on an equal footing will ensure that the mistakes of the past will not be repeated and that the new archaeology and the new quest for Jesus can be mutually enriching for each other.

BIBLIOGRAPHY

Adan-Bayewitz, D. (1993) *Common Pottery in Roman Galilee: A study in local trade*, Ramat Gan: Bar Illan University Press.

Adan-Bayewitz, D. and Perlman, I. (1990) 'The local trade of Sepphoris in the Roman period', *IEJ* 19, 153–72.

Adan-Bayewitz, D. and Wieder, M. (1992) 'Ceramics from Galilee: a comparison of several techniques for fabric characterisation', *JFA* 19, 189–205.

Alt, A. (1953–64) 'Galiläische Probleme, 1937–40', in *Kleine Schriften zur Geschichte des Volkes Israels*, 3 vols, Munich: C. Beck, vol. 2, 363–435.

—— (1949) 'Die Stätten des Wirkens Jesu in Galiläa Territorial-geschichtlich Betrachtet', *Kleine Schriften zur Geschichte des Volkes Israels*, 3 vols, Munich: C. Beck, vol. 2, 436–55.

Applebaum, S. (1986) 'The settlement pattern of western Samaria from Hellenistic to Byzantine times: a historical commentary', in S. Dar, *Landscape and Pattern: An Archaeological survey of Samaria, 800 B.C.E.–636 C.E.*, *BAR International Series* 308 (i), 257– 69.

Aviam, M. (1985) 'The Roman temple in Kedesh in the light of certain northern Syrian city coins', *TA* 12, 212–14.

—— (1993) 'Galilee: the Hellenistic and Byzantine periods', in E. Stern (ed.) *The New Encylopaedia of Archaeological Excavations of the Holy Land*, 4 vols, Jerusalem: The Israel Exploration Society, vol. 2, 452–8.

Avi-Yonah, M. (1951) 'Mount Carmel and the god of Baalbeck', *IEJ* 2, 118–24.

—— (1959) 'Syrian gods at Ptolemais-Acho', *IEJ* 9, 1–12.

—— (1966) *The Holy Land from the Persian to the Arab Conquest: An historical geography*, Grand Rapids, Mich.: Baker Books.

Bagatti, B. (1971) *Antichi villaggi Christani di Galilea*, Jerusalem: Franciscan Biblical Publications, Collectio Minor, N.13.

Barag, D. (1982–3) 'Tyrian currency in Galilee', *INJ* 67, 7–13.

Barker, G. and Lloyd, J. (eds) (1991) *Roman Landscapes: Archaeological Surveys in the Mediterranean region*, Archaeological Monographs of the British School at Rome 2, London: British School at Rome.

Batey, R. (1984a) 'Is not this the carpenter?', *NTS* 30, 249–58.

—— (1984b) 'Jesus and the theatre', *NTS* 30, 563–74.

—— (1991) *Jesus and the Forgotten City: New light on Sepphoris and the urban world of Jesus*, Grand Rapids, Mich.: Baker Books.

Bauer, W. (1927) 'Jesus der Galiläer', in G. Strecker (ed.) (1967), *Kleine Schriften zur Geschichte des Volkes Israels*, Tübingen: J. C. B. Mohr, 91–108.

Ben-David, A. (1969) *Jerusalem und Tyros: ein Beitrag zur Palästinensischen Münz- und Wirtschaftsgeschichte*, Basel: Kyklos-Verlag.

Bertram, W. (1935) 'Der Hellenismus in der Urheimat des Evangeliums', *ARW*, 265–81.

Betz, H. D. (1994) 'Jesus and the Cynics: Survey and analysis of an hypo-thesis', *JR* 74, 453–75.

Biran, A. (1981) 'To the god who is in Dan', in A. Biran (ed.) *Temples and High Places in Biblical Times*, Jerusalem: Hebrew Union College–Jewish Institute of Religion, 142–51.

Borg, M. (1994) *Jesus in Contemporary Scholarship*, Valley Forge, Pa.: Trinity Press International.

Case, S. (1926) 'Jesus and Sepphoris', *JBL* 45, 14–22.

Carney, T. F. (1975) *The Shape of the Past: Models in antiquity*, Lawrence, Kan.: Coronado Press.

Chilton, B. (1992) *The Temple of Jesus: His sacrificial program within a cultural history of sacrifice*, Philadelphia, Pa.: Pennsylvania State University Press.

Conder, C. R. and Kitchener, A. H. (1881) *The Survey of Western Palestine 1, Sheets I–VI, Galilee*, London: Palestine Exploration Fund.

Crossan, J. D. (1991) *The Historical Jesus: The life of a Mediterranean Jewish peasant*, New York and San Francisco: Harper.

Dalman. G. (1924) *Orte und Wege Jesu*, Gütersloh: Gerd Mohn.

Danby, M. (1993) *The Mishnah*, Oxford: Oxford University Press.

Dar, S. (1986) *Landscape and Pattern: An archaeological survey of Samaria, 800 BCE–636 CE*, 2 vols, *BAR International Series*, 308 i and ii.

—— (1993) *Settlements and Cult Sites on Mount Hermon, Israel: Iturean culture in the Hellenistic and Roman periods*, *BAR International Series* 589.

Dauphin, C. and Schonfield J. (1983) 'Settlements of the Roman and Byzantine periods on the Golan heights', *IEJ* 33, 189–206.

Dauphin, C. and Gibson, S. (1992–3) 'Ancient settlements and their land-scapes: the results of ten years of survey on the Golan heights (1978–8)', *BAIAS* 12, 7–31.

Diakonoff, I. M. (1992) 'The naval power and trade of Tyre', *IEJ* 42, 168–93.

Downing, G. (1992) *Cynics and Christian Origins*, Edinburgh: T. and T. Clark.

Duncan-Jones, R. (1994) *Money and Government in the Roman Empire*, Cambridge: Cambridge University Press.

Edwards, D. (1988) 'First-century rural–urban relations in Lower Galilee: exploring the archaeological evidence', in D. Lull (ed.) *SBLASP*, Atlanta: Scholars Press, 169–82.

—— (1992) 'The socio-economic and cultural ethos of Lower Galilee in the first century: implications for the nascent Jesus Movement', in L. Levine (ed.) *The Galilee in Late Antiquity*, New York and Jerusalem: The Jewish Theological Seminary of America, 53–74.

Elliot, J. (1993) *What is Social-scientific Criticism?*, Minneapolis: Fortress Press.

Epstein, C. and Gutmann, S. (1972) 'The survey in the Golan heights', in M. Kochavi (ed.) *Judea, Samaria and the Golan: Archaeological Survey 1967–8*, Jerusalem: Archaeological Survey of Israel, 243–98 (Hebrew).

Esler, P. (1994) *The First Christians in their Social Worlds*, London and New York: Routledge.

—— (1995) *Modeling Early Christianity: Social Scientific Studies of the New Testament in its Context*, London and New York: Routledge.

Fiensey, D. (1991) *The Social History of Palestine in the Herodian Period*, Lewiston and Lampeter: The Edwin Mellen Press.

Finley, M. (1977) *The Ancient Economy*, 2nd edition, London: Chatto and Windus.

—— (1981) 'The ancient city: from Fustel de Coulanges to Max Weber and beyond', *CSSH* 19, 305–27.

Fischer, M., Ovadiah, A. and Roll, I. (1984) 'The Roman temple at Kedesh, Upper Galilee: a preliminary study', *TA* 11, 147–72.

—— (1986) 'The epigraphic finds from the Roman temple at Kedesh in the Upper Galilee', *TA* 13, 60–6.

Frankel, R. (1989–90) 'Har Mizpe Yamim 1988–9', *ESI* 9, 100–2.

—— (1992) 'Some oil-presses from western Galilee', *BASOR* 286, 39–71.

Freyne, S. (1980) *Galilee from Alexander the Great to Hadrian: A study of Second Temple Judaism*, Wilmington, Del.: Michael Glazier and Notre Dame University Press.

—— (1987) 'Galilee–Jerusalem relations according to Josephus' *Vita*', *NTS*, 600–9.

—— (1988a) *Galilee, Jesus and the Gospels: Literary approaches and historical investigations*, Dublin and Minneapolis: Gill and Macmillan and Augsburg-Fortress.

—— (1988b) 'Bandits in Galilee: a contribution to the study of social conditions in first-century Galilee', in J. Neusner, J. Neuser, E. S. Frerichs and R. Horsley (eds) *The Social World of Formative Christianity and Judaism: Essays in tribute of Howard Clark Kee*, Philadelphia: Fortress Press, 50–69.

—— (1994) 'The geography, politics and economics of Galilee and the quest for the historical Jesus', in B. Chilton and C. Evans (eds) *Studying the Historical Jesus: Evaluations of the current state of the research*, Leiden: Brill, 75–124.

—— (1995a) 'Jesus and the urban culture of Galilee', in T. Fornberg and D. Hellholm (eds) *Texts and Contexts. Texts in their Textual and Situational Contexts: Essays in honour of Lars Hartman*, Oslo, Copenhagen, Stockholm, Boston: Scandinavia University Press, 597–622.

—— (1995b) 'Herodian economics in Galilee: searching for a suitable model', in P. Esler (ed.) *Modeling Early Christianity: Social scientific studies of the New Testament in its context*, London and New York: Routledge, 23–46.

Gal, Z. (1992) *Lower Galilee during the Iron Age*, ASORDS, vol. 8, Winona Lake, Ind.: Eisenbrauns.

Guérin, V. (1868–80) *Description géographique, historique et archéologique de la Palestine, Galilee*, Paris.

Grundman, W. (1941) *Jesus der Galiläer und das Judentum*, Leipzig.

Gutmann, S. and Wagner, D. (1986–7) 'Gamla, 1984, 1985, 1986', *ESI* 5, 38–41.

Hanson, R. (1980) *Tyrian Influence in the Upper Galilee*, Cambridge, Mass.: ASOR Publications.

Hartel, M. (1987) 'Khirbet Zemel 1985–6', *IEJ* 37, 270–2.

—— (1989) *Northern Golan Heights: The archaeological survey as a source of local history*, Qazrin: Israel Department of Antiquities and Museums, Ministry of Education and Culture (Hebrew).

Hopkins, K. (1980) 'Economic growth and towns in classical antiquity', in P. Abrams and E. Wrigley (eds) *Towns in Societies: Essays in economic history and historical sociology*, Cambridge: Cambridge University Press, 35–77.

Horsley, R. (1994) 'The historical Jesus and archaeology of the Galilee: questions from historical Jesus research to archaeologists', in D. Lull (ed.) *SBLASP*, Atlanta: Scholars Press, 91–135.

Ilan, Z. (1993) 'Meroth', in E. Stern (ed.) *The New Encylopaedia of Archaeological Excavations in the Holy Land*, 4 vols, Jerusalem: The Israel Exploration Society, vol. 3, 1028–31.

Ilan, Z. (1986–7) 'Galilee, survey of synagogues', *ESI* 5, 35–7.

Josephus, trans. H. St J. Thackeray and R. Marcus (1956–65), Loeb Classical Library, London: Heinemann; Cambridge, Mass.: Harvard University Press.

Kasher, A. (1988) *Jews, Idumeans, and ancient Arabs*, Tübingen: J. C. B. Mohr.

Kee, H. (1980) *Christian Origins in Sociological Perspective*, London: SCM Press.

Klein, C. (1978) *Anti-Judaism in Christian Theology*, London: SPCK.

Lang, F. (1978) 'Über Sidon mittens ins Gebiet der Dekapolis: Geographie und Theologie in Markus 7:31', *ZDPV* 94, 145–59.

Levine, L. (ed.) (1992) *The Galilee in Late Antiquity*, New York and Jerusalem: The Jewish Theological Seminary of America.

Lull, D. (ed.) (1994) *SBLASP*, Atlanta, Scholars Press.

Mack, B. (1988) *A Myth of Innocence: Mark and Christian origins*, Philadelphia: Fortress Press.

—— (1993) *The Lost Gospel: The Book of Q and Christian origins*, New York, San Francisco: Harper.

McMullen, R. (1970) 'Market days in the Roman Empire', *Phoenix* 24, 333–41.

Malina, B. and Rohrbaugh, R. (1992) *A Social-scientific Commentary on the Synoptic Gospels*, Minneapolis: Fortress Press.

Malherbe, A. (1977) *Social Aspects of Early Christianity*, Baton Rouge: Louisiana State University.

Ma'oz, Z. (1992) 'The synagogue in the Second Temple period: architectural and social interpretation', *EI* 22, 331–44 (Hebrew).

Marxsen, W. (1956) *Der Evangelist Markus: Studien zur Redaktionsgeschichte des Evangeliums, FRLANT* 67, Göttingen: Vandenhoeck and Ruprecht.

Meeks, W. (1983) *The First Urban Christians*, New Haven and London: Yale University Press.

Meier, J. (1991) *A Marginal Jew: Rethinking the Historical Jesus*, New York: Doubleday.

Meshorer, Y. (1985) *City Coins of Eretz Israel and the Dekapolis in the Roman Period*, Jerusalem: The Israel Museum.

Meyers, E. (1976) 'Galilean regionalism as a factor in historical reconstruction', *BASOR* 221, 95–101.

—— (1985) 'Galilean regionalism: a reappraisal', in W. Scott Green (ed.) *Approaches to Ancient Judaism and its Greco-Roman Context*, Atlanta, Scholars Press.

—— (1986) 'Sepphoris, the ornament of all Galilee', *BA* 49, 4–19.

—— (1992) 'Roman Sepphoris in the light of new archaeological evidence and recent research', in L. Levine, (ed.) *The Galilee in Late Antiquity*, 321–38.

—— (1993) 'Nabratein', in E. Stern (ed.) *The New Encylopaedia of Archaeological Excavations in the Holy Land*, Jerusalem: The Israel Exploration Society vol. 3, 1077–9.

Meyers, E. and Meyers, C. (1989) 'Expanding the frontiers of biblical archaeology', *EI* 20, Yigael Yadin Volume, 140*–7* .

Meyers, E. and Strange, J. (1981) *Archaeology, the Rabbis and Early Christianity*, London and Nashville: SCM and John Knox Press.

Meyers, E., Netzer, E. and Meyers, C. (1992) *Sepphoris*, Winona Lake, Ind: Eisenbrauns.

Meyers, E., Strange, J. and Groh, D. (1978) 'The Meiron excavation project: archaeological survey in Galilee and Golan, 1976', *BASOR* 230, 1–24.

Netzer, E. and Weiss, Z. (1994) *Zippori*, Jerusalem: The Israel Exploration Society.

Neyrey, J. (ed.) (1991) *The Social World of Luke–Acts*, Peabody, Mass.: Hendrickson.

Nun, M. (1988) *Ancient Anchorages and Harbours around the Sea of Galilee*, Ein Gev: Kibbutz Kinneret Publications.

Oakman, D. (1986) *Jesus and the Economic Questions of his Day*, Lewison and Lampeter: The Edwin Mellen Press.

—— (1994) 'The archaeology of first-century Galilee and the social interpretation of the historical Jesus', in D. Lull, (ed.) *SBLASP*, Atlanta: Scholars Press, 221–51.

Oppenheimer, A. (1977) *The 'am ha-aretz: A study in the social history of the Jewish people in the Hellenistic and Roman periods*, Leiden: Brill.

Overman, A. (1988) 'Who were the first urban Christians? Urbanisation in first-century Galilee', in D. Lull (ed.) *SBLASP*, Atlanta: Scholars Press, 160–8.

—— (1993) 'Recent advances in in the archaeology of the Galilee in the Roman period', in A. Hauser and P. Sellew (eds) *Current Research in Biblical Studies*, Sheffield: JSOT Press, 35–58.

Raynor, J. and Meshorer, Y. (1988) *The Coins of Ancient Meiron*, Winona Lake, Ind.: Eisenbrauns.

Renan, E. (1863) *La vie de Jésus*, English translation, New York: Prometheus Books, 1991.

Rich, J. and Wallace-Hadrill, A. (eds) (1991) *Town and Country in Antiquity*, London and New York: Routledge.

Roll, I. (1983) 'The Roman road system in Judea', *The Jerusalem Cathedra* 3, 136–81.

—— (1993) 'Roman roads', in Y. Tsafrir, L. Di Segni and J. Green (eds) *Tabula Imperii Romani. Iudea–Palestina*, Jerusalem: The Israel Academy of the Sciences, 21–2, with detailed map.

Sanders, E. (1984) *Jesus and Judaism*, London: SCM Press.

Sawicki, M. (1995) 'Archaeology as space technology: digging for gender and class in the Holy Land', in *Method and Theory in the Study of Religion*, Berlin: de Gruyter, 319–48.

Schmeller, T. (1994) 'Jesus im Umland Galiläas: zu den Markinischen Berichten vom Aufenthalt Jesu in den Gebieten von Tyros, Caesarea-Philippi und der Dekapolis', *BZ* 38, 44–66.

Schürer, E. (1886, revised edn 1979) *The History of the Jewish People in the Age of Jesus Christ*, vols I–IV, revision and translation of the second

German edition by G. Vermes, F. Miller and M. Black, Edinburgh: T. and T. Clark.

Scott, E. (ed.) (1993) *Theoretical Roman Archaeology: First conference proceedings* (Worldwide Archaeology Series), Aldershot: Avebury.

Smith, J. Z. (1975) 'The social description of early Christianity', *RelStRev* 1, 19–25.

Stern, E. (ed.) (1993) *The New Encylopaedia of Archaeological Excavations in the Holy Land*, 4 vols, Jerusalem: The Israel Exploration Society.

Strange, J. (1992a) 'Six campaigns at Sepphoris: the University of South Florida excavations, 1983–9', in L. Levine, (ed.) *The Galilee in Late Antiquity*, 339–56.

—— (1992b) 'Some implications of archaeology for New Testament studies', in J. H. Charlesworth (ed.) *What has Archaeology to do with Faith?*, Philadelphia: Fortress Press.

—— (1994) 'First-century Galilee from archaeology and from texts', in D. Lull (ed.) *SBLSP*, Atlanta: Scholars Press, 81–90.

Strange, J. F., Groh, D. E. and Longstaff, T. R. W. (1994) 'Excavations at Sepphoris: the location and identification of Shikhin. Part 1', *IEJ* 44, 216–27.

Sussman, J. (1981) 'The inscription in the synagogue in Rehob', in L. Levine (ed.) *Ancient Synagogues Revealed*, Jerusalem: The Israel Exploration Society, 146–53.

Theissen G. (1983) *Studien zur Soziologie des Urchristentums*, Tübingen: J. C. B. Mohr.

—— (1992) *The Gospels in Context: Social and political history in the synoptic tradition*, Edinburgh: T. and T. Clark.

Tzaferis, V. (1992a) 'Cults and deities worshipped at Caesarea-Philippi (Banias)', in J. W. Wright, R. P. Carroll and P. R. Davies (eds) *Priests, Prophets and Scribes: Essays on the formation and heritage of Second Temple Judaism in Honour of Joseph Blenkinsopp*, JSOT Supplement series 149, Sheffield, JSOT Press.

—— (1992b) The ' "god who is in Dan" and the cult of Pan at Banias in the Hellenistic and Roman periods', *EI* 23, A. Biran Volume, Jerusalem: The Israel Exploration Society, 128*–35*.

Urman, D. (1985) *The Golan: A profile of a region during the Roman and Byzantine periods*, Oxford: BAR International Series, 269.

Vale, R. (1987) 'Literary sources in archaeological description: the case of Galilee, Galilees and Galileans', *JSJ* 18, 210–28.

Vitto, F. (1983–4) 'A look into the workshop of a Late Roman Galilean potter', *BAIAS* 19–22.

Wallace-Hadrill, A. (1991) 'Elites and trade in the Roman town', in J. Rich and A. Wallace-Hadrill (eds) *City and Country in the Ancient World*, London and New York: Routledge, 241–72.

Whittaker, C. R. (1991) 'The consumer city revisited: the *vicus* and the city', *JRA* 3, 110–18.

ON THE PILGRIM'S WAY TO THE HOLY CITY OF JERUSALEM

The basilica of Dor in Israel

Claudine Dauphin

Long before the advent of Christianity, the city of Jerusalem had become a focal point of religious attention. The Jews regarded it as the 'centre of the world' and the 'navel of the earth', and Pliny's description of Jerusalem as 'by far the most famous of the cities of the east' (*Natural History* V, 70) bears witness to its fame outside Palestine prior to the Jewish Wars of the first and second centuries CE. The temple of Jerusalem, built on the site of the covenant of Abraham, had been first destroyed in 586 BCE by Nebuchednezzar, rebuilt under Cyrus in 538 BCE, and enlarged and transformed by Herod the Great (37 BCE–4 CE). It lay at the heart of the religious life of the Jews. Perhaps as many as half a million Jews flocked there three times a year to make their biblically ordained offerings, since prayer in synagogue was instituted as a substitute only later. The Acts of the Apostles (2:5–11) describes vividly one of these festivals: the feast of Shavuot or Pentecost, which commemorated Moses copying the Law at God's dictation on Mount Sinai. The city of Jerusalem overflowed then with pilgrims 'out of every nation under heaven'. The quelling of the first Jewish revolt against Rome culminated in the capture and destruction of Jerusalem in 70 CE by the Roman legions of Titus. Its Jewish population was expelled from Judaea, the area around Jerusalem, and was forbidden by the Romans to remain in the south. Jerusalem, however, retained its role as spiritual magnet, and both rabbinic and Christian pilgrim sources mention the Jews' annual return to the City to lament at the site of the Temple.

145

JERUSALEM, FOCUS OF CHRISTIAN PILGRIMAGE

For the Christians, too, Jerusalem held a very special place. It was the site of the culmination of Christ's ministry on earth and of the birth of the Christian church. At Pentecost, seven weeks after his crucifixion, the Holy Spirit had inspired the apostles to preach the Gospels and to put into action Christ's command: 'Go therefore and make disciples of all nations' (Matt 28:19). The local church of Jerusalem looked to James, the Lord's brother, as its first bishop, and laid claim to a position of great prestige in early Christendom. Its pre-eminent status was officially recognised only in the fifth century, when it became one of the five patriarchates. As early as the beginning of the fourth century, Christian pilgrims were already assembling from all over the world to visit the 'Upper Room' on Mount Zion (the traditional site of the Last Supper) , the Pools of Bethesda and Siloam which figured in the New Testament narratives, the rock on the Mount of Olives where Christ had ascended to heaven and which bore his footprints and, close by, the grotto where he taught his disciples. From the Mount of Olives, too, they could be shown the fulfilment of the prophecy of Christ in the destruction of the Jewish city: 'Do you see these great buildings? There will not be left here one stone upon another, that will not be thrown down' (Mark 13:2). The statues of the presiding deities of the Roman pagan Aelia Capitolina – Jupiter Capitolinus and the deified Emperor Hadrian whose family name was 'Aelius' – now dominated the site of the ruined temple.

On 28 October 312 the Roman Emperor Constantine defeated his rival Maxentius at the Milvian Bridge. He attributed the victory to the intervention of the God of the Christians and this spurred him into adopting Christianity as the official religion of the Roman Empire. This changed the status of Palestine from a provincial backwater to the Holy Land, the centre of worship, economically pampered by the emperors. Driven by a sense of mission, Constantine had Aelia Capitolina razed to the ground 'by the command of God', eventually to reveal the cave which, to the Jerusalem Christians, was the place of Christ's resurrection. Christian pilgrims could now *see* the tomb that bore witness to the resurrection of the Saviour; they were faced with physical facts more telling than any words. By opening up the Sepulchre and ordering the bishop of Jerusalem to erect a basilica over it, Constantine seized the opportunity both to glorify his Lord and to create at the same time a symbolic centre of the faith of the Empire.

Adorned and encircled with columns, the Holy Sepulchre became, so to speak, the 'head' of the metaphorical body of buildings described by Eusebius, Bishop of Caesarea, in the biography of Emperor Constantine the Great his contemporary, which he entitled the *Vita Constantini*. The complex of the Holy Sepulchre has seen such vicissitudes and transformations since the fourth century that a variety of different restorations of the original buildings have been proposed. The salient points of these buildings can be gathered from Eusebius' description, and the picture can be occasionally sharpened with the aid of archaeology. Proceeding eastwards from the Sepulchre itself, which was to become the church of the Anastasis, one came to a large, open, paved court with long colonnades on each side and at the far end. In the south-eastern corner of this court was situated the rock of Golgotha, the actual site of the crucifixion. On the side of the court opposite the Sepulchre was built the basilica, the Martyrium of Golgotha (Gibson and Taylor 1994: 75, figure 45). Eusebius was impressed by the great height of this basilica, the huge columns and galleries, the gilded ceiling – at its head was a 'hemisphere' decorated with twelve columns surmounted by silver bowls, the personal gift of Constantine. The basilica had three entrances at its eastern end, which opened from another colonnaded *atrium* or forecourt. The main entrance to the buildings, the *propylea*, opened onto the main street of Aelia, affording to passersby a splendid view of the magnificent new buildings, and their adornments of gold, silver and precious stones.

The dedication of the Holy Sepulchre complex coincided with Constantine's *Tricennalia* in 335 – the celebration of thirty years of reign. Thus, the Emperor's personal fortunes were intertwined with those of the Holy Land. Constantine's interest in Palestine was shared by other members of his family, particularly his mother Helena, whose pilgrimage in 326 led to the founding of churches and the distribution of charity. Helena supervised the building of basilicas on the Mount of Olives, over the grotto where Christ was reputed to have taught the disciples – the Eleona Church – and at the cave of the nativity in Bethlehem. The Constantinian nucleus in the Church of the Nativity consisted of a roughly square basilica paved with magnificent geometric mosaics, preceded by a huge colonnaded *atrium* covering a much greater area than the basilica itself.

On the sixth-century mosaic map of Palestine that paved the floor of a church in Madaba in Transjordan, Jerusalem holds a dominant position (Avi-Yonah 1954: 50–60, plate 7, nos 52–3). The colonnaded main street of Hadrian's Aelia Capitolina, the *cardo maximus*, is clearly visible, running southwards from what is now the Damascus Gate in the direction of Mount Zion, which lay outside the southern city wall until changes brought to the line of the city wall at the time of the Empress Eudocia in the middle of the fifth century. In a distinguished central position on the west side of this street, breaking the colonnade, are the steps leading to the *propylea* of Constantine's basilica; its three doorways are clearly visible. The complex of buildings on Golgotha is the largest edifice depicted, and is clearly meant to be seen as the focal point of the city, culminating in the domed rotunda which by that date covered the Holy Sepulchre. The steps leading directly to the main entrance of the basilica off the street recall Eusebius' description of its fronting onto the main thoroughfare.

The deliberate emphasis on the central position of the Constantinian buildings at Jerusalem on the Madaba map reflects the importance of the Constantinian foundations. If Jerusalem was for the Christians the centre of the world, then the centre of Jerusalem itself could only be the place of Christ's death and resurrection. By contrast with the church of the 'Upper Room' where the Jerusalem community had worshipped down the ages, tucked away outside the city on Mount Zion, Constantine's Holy Sepulchre was on the site of the Hadrianic *temenos*, alongside the forum and near the central crossroads, approached by an impressive flight of steps from the main thoroughfare; the new Christian monuments, and no longer the pagan temples, were the highlights of the city.

Thus fourth-century Jerusalem saw Christianity symbolically transported from its place outside the walls to the very heart of the city. Roman Aelia was now the Christian Jerusalem. It was Constantine's creation of the 'new Jerusalem' of Rev 21:2 – 'And I John saw the holy city, new Jerusalem, coming down from God out of heaven, prepared as a bride adorned for her husband' – which lay at the heart of the Holy Land's emergence as a goal of pilgrimage in the fourth century (Hunt 1982).

THE PILGRIM'S PROGRESS

To this 'new Jerusalem' pilgrims flocked from all over the Empire to worship at the holy places adorned with imported marbles, precious stones, gold and silver. St John had prophesied:

And the building of the wall of it was of jasper: and the city was pure gold, like unto clear glass. . . . And the foundations of the wall of the city were garnished with all manner of precious stones. . . . And the twelve gates were twelve pearls; and the street of the city was pure gold, as it were transparent glass.

(Revelation 21:18–21)

But this bejewelled crown of the Holy Land was reached only after an arduous journey on land or sea. Pilgrims braved long delays, storms and shipwreck as they embarked on merchant ships plying to and fro between the west and Syro-Palestine. The coastal ports of Syria and Palestine – Ascalon and Gaza for instance – were active and prosperous. From here were exported the local produce of Palestine – textiles from Bet She'an-Scythopolis, and wines and dates from the southern *limes* or frontier and the Negev desert – as well as goods from Arabia which arrived by caravan routes. That Gaza wine, *gazetum* or *gazetinum*, was exported to the west is suggested both by its mention by western writers, Isidorus, Marcus Aurelius, Cassiodorus and Sidonius Apollinaris, and by the discovery of typical Gaza *amphorae* on excavation sites dated between the fourth and sixth centuries CE in North Africa and Gaul. Pilgrims could cut travelling time by sailing to Syria via Alexandria, making use of the north-westerly winds and crossing into Palestine on land at the Ladder of Tyre – a huge chalk barrier in southern Phoenicia – or even sailing to Alexandria, visiting the monastic communities of the Egyptian deserts and then proceeding up to Jerusalem by the land-route. These were quicker than the direct route across the Mediterranean. Furthermore, reaching the port of Alexandria was made particularly simple by the grain-ships returning empty after their voyages to Rome or Constantinople. By ship, the Holy Land was within a fortnight's sail of Rome, or three weeks from Gaul. But sea-voyagers had to endure difficult conditions. Since ships primarily carried merchandise, passengers had to find quarters on the deck where they were exposed to the elements, while their luggage went into the hold with the cargo.

None of this discomfort would have been felt by members of the senatorial class, who progressed in leisurely fashion across the Mediterranean in their own flotilla of boats with a party of bishops, priests, eunuchs and Moorish slaves, and frequently stopped *en route* in Sicily, Greece, Rhodes and Cyprus, to visit ancient sites and

CLAUDINE DAUPHIN

high-ranking ecclesiastical friends. Some other pilgrims were so poor
that they could not afford the sea-passage: monks for instance who
had no money of their own. They worked their passage or were
lucky sometimes to find a sympathetic captain. St Jerome tells how
the monk Hilarion, a calligrapher by trade, offered the captain a
copy of the Scriptures to secure his passage.

Although monks and pilgrims hastened to the Holy Land from
Mesopotamia and even farther eastwards – St Jerome daily received
in his monastery at Bethlehem monks from India, Persia and
Ethiopia – pilgrimage is best documented from the west. From
Constantinople, pilgrims followed the 'Pilgrim's Road' across Asia
Minor to Tarsus and Antioch in Cilicia, or approached the Holy
Land from the port of Alexandria. In all cases, they travelled along
the great coast road linking Antioch and Alexandria – the *Via Maris*.

Standing on this road at Caesarea, Jerusalem lay only 73 Roman
miles, or three days' journey away. On an average day, and on a
journey of some length, the pilgrims travelled some 20 to 25 Roman
miles, as may be calculated from the detailed record of the Pilgrim
of Bordeaux on his road from Gaul to Jerusalem. He left Chalcedon
on the eastern shore of the Sea of Marmara, which lies between
Constantinople and the Dardanelles, on 30 May 333, and arrived
back in Constantinople on 26 December of the same year. He was
thus away from the capital for seven months. On his way to
Jerusalem, he passed through fifty-eight hostels or *mansiones*.
Assuming that he stayed a night at each one, he took a little over
eight weeks on the 1,200-mile journey from Constantinople to
Jerusalem, an average of 21 miles per day. Pilgrims, except for a few
privileged ones, were not permitted to use the Imperial Post, the
cursus publicus: the Byzantine Law Codes are full of strictures against
the use of the facilities by private citizens. One of those privileged
pilgrims was Gregory, Bishop of Nyssa in Cappadocia, who was
granted the privilege of travelling by the *cursus publicus* when he
journeyed to Jerusalem in 379. This honour, bestowed by the
Emperor himself, is no doubt to be accounted for by the fact that
Gregory was a bishop who had been attending a church council,
and whose journey to Jerusalem combined pilgrimage and ecclesiastical business.

No pilgrim could escape the sophisticated organisation of staging
posts for change of mounts (*mutationes*) or for overnight stay
(*mansiones*) which the *cursus publicus* had imposed on the major
routes of the Empire. The Roman or Byzantine *mansio*, like its

successor the *khan* or caravanserai of the Turkish caravan routes, consisted of a large courtyard with facilities for feeding and stabling animals, surrounded by rooms where travellers ate and rested, the sleeping quarters being situated on the first floor. If the *mansio* was full, the pilgrims had to join other travellers in the local inn (or *taverna*). *Mansiones* and *tavernae* enjoyed no better reputation among 'respectable' Christians than they had done among the pagan Roman upper classes, and the clergy in particular were forbidden by ecclesiastical canons to enter those establishments, which Gregory of Nyssa saw as a danger, a source of possible corruption to Christian pilgrims. To cater for the needs of Christian travellers, resthouses of an ecclesiastical nature, official hostels or *xenodochia*, supervised by members of the clergy and often associated with monasteries, soon sprang up in towns along the main pilgrim routes. In the 380s Gregory of Nyssa described them as scattered all over the eastern provinces and by 437 the route between Constantinople and Jerusalem was well supplied with *pandocheia* – inns specifically for pilgrims.

Nevertheless, the route presented hardships, especially for pilgrims who had adopted an ascetic diet, which undermined their resistance to the stress of travel and climatic changes. In 437, Melania the Younger fought her way through deep snow on her way from Constantinople to Jerusalem. Summer travellers had to face dry, dusty conditions in Anatolia followed by the intense humid heat of coastal Cilicia. This combination proved too much for Jerome on his first trip to the east in 374. He survived, but his companion Innocentius died on reaching Antioch. Most of the journeys undertaken by pilgrims in Egypt and Palestine were in desert regions, unfamiliar terrain for a Melania or an Egeria who had been brought up in the sheltered life of the western aristocracy, a class which intensely abhorred the discomforts of travel. Egeria, the abbess of a monastery in Galicia in north-western Spain, travelled to the Holy Land in 381–4. She overcame the labour of reaching the summit of Mount Sinai on foot and climbed Mount Nebo on donkey and foot, sustained, she affirms in her diary, by her unremitting *locorum sanctorum desiderium*, her yearning for the holy places, throughout her physical and spiritual peregrination to the Holy City (*Itinerarium Egeriae* 3; Pétré 1948: 102–5).

This *desiderium*, which led pilgrims up mountains and into the deserts, was a longing to see with one's own eyes the scenes of events which were so familiar from the Bible, and yet had seemed so remote as long as the Roman Empire had been officially pagan.

The 'travel-kit' of pilgrims included two main items: the Bible and guide-books based on the *Onomastikon*, a descriptive list of sites in Palestine compiled by Eusebius, Bishop of Caesarea, and translated from Greek into Latin around 390 by Jerome, who had himself travelled widely in the Holy Land and Egypt. Bible and guide-books in hand, and often accompanied by pilgrim guides who tended to feed the gullible with mistaken locations and romantic stories, the pilgrims punctuated their approach to Jerusalem by visiting sites connected with the scriptures. They worshipped at the shrines of local saints: notably, Elijah on Mount Carmel on the coastal road to Caesarea, and inland, Jacob's town of Shechem, where Joseph was buried and Sychar, the place of Jacob's well and of Christ's meeting with the Samaritan woman. One of these stop-overs for pilgrims along the *Via Maris* on the way to Jerusalem, was the episcopal basilica of Dora, which we have been excavating since 1979.[1]

THE EPISCOPAL BASILICA OF DOR, CENTRE OF PILGRIMAGE AND HEALING

The revival of the ancient Hebrew name of 'Dor' at the time of the foundation of the State of Israel in 1948, reflects the antiquity of the site. The word 'Dor' is related to the Babylonian *Du-ru* meaning 'a place or fortress surrounded by a wall or rampart'. Thirty km south of Haifa and 10 km north of Caesarea on the Mediterranean coast, a massive mound or tell juts out into the Mediterranean Sea. It is the result of the accumulation of layers of human occupation since the fifteenth century BCE when Dor was one of the thirty-one fortified Canaanite cities conquered by Joshua. Later, on the coins of Trajan and Hadrian, Dora was called 'the holy autonomous city, with the right of sanctuary, mistress of a fleet'. According to the Jewish Roman historian Flavius Josephus, it had in the first century CE a Jewish minority large enough to maintain a synagogue. It appears to have declined in Imperial times, in the second and third centuries CE. In Jerome's *Onomastikon*, fourth-century Dora is described as 'a city now deserted' (Klostermann 1904: 250.56), and in *Epistle* 108, dated to 404, in connection with the pilgrim Paula's first journey round the sites of Palestine in 385, Jerome writes: 'She marvelled in the ruins of Dor, a city once very powerful' (Wilkinson 1977: 47). Both comments have, in the past, too often been understood literally. They are rather to be judged in the light of Jerome's interest in sites as fossilised embodiments of biblical events. That Dora was an episcopal see, first suffragant of adjacent Caesarea, metropolis of the archepiscopal see of *Palaestina Prima*, were not worth a mention by Jerome, since his *Onomastikon* aimed not to describe contemporary cities, but merely indicated to pilgrims biblical archaeological remains worth visiting. The mention of Dora in Byzantine geographical treatises and the reports of its bishops' attendance at Church Councils throughout the sixth and seventh centuries bear witness to its historical importance in the Byzantine period. The population abandoned the summit of the tell in the Late Roman period, and the Byzantine settlement grew on its north-eastern slope and at its foot. This site was also chosen by Jewish colonists from Turkey and Russia to establish Kibbutz Nahsholim in 1948, once they had wrenched control of the bay of Dor from the Bedouin Arabs who had settled there in the fifteenth century, renaming it Tanturah.

In the course of preparing the area for the construction of new houses at Kibbutz Nahsholim, ancient remains came to light. This called for a rescue excavation, conducted in February 1952 by Dr J. Leibovitch on behalf of the Israel Department of Antiquities and Museums. The semi-circular eastward-oriented apse of the central nave of a large basilica was cleared, as was part of the mosaic pavement of a northern aisle. Besides the impressive size of the building, one find in particular supported Leibovitch's assertion that this was the episcopal basilica of Byzantine Dora. An episcopal ivory sceptre lacking its handle was discovered. It was shaped like a hand, the three middle fingers extended in a characteristic episcopal blessing symbolizing the Holy Trinity. One of the fingers bore an ivory ring. The excavations were discontinued after the illness and death of Leibovitch, and the site was abandoned. Some members of Kibbutz Nahsholim, whose houses had been built close to the church, gradually took it over, in defiance of the Antiquities Law, and planted palm trees in the nave, rose-bushes in the central apse, and transformed the area into a shrubbery. The mosaics, overgrown and everywhere penetrated by roots, were threatened with total disappearance. The site was sufficiently important for the then Israel Department of Antiquities and Museums (now the Israel Antiquities Authority) to reinitiate the excavations of the church at Dor.[2]

The Byzantine church complex at Dor is huge (figure 7.1), covering at least 1,000 square metres, and it stands on a vast raised platform, edged on the north and west by roads which still exist as paths. It is thus one of the largest ecclesiastical complexes excavated in Israel outside of Jerusalem.

Figure 7.1 Dor church: general view from the north-west
(photo Z. Radovan)

The core of the structure consisted of a three-aisled basilica, 18.5 m long and 14 m wide (plan, figure 7.2). The central nave, which terminated in the east in a semi-circular apse, was flanked by side-aisles. The walls were built of ashlars occasionally laid as headers and stretchers and internally plastered. In some places, the plaster has survived on the upper faces of the foundation course, this suggesting that courses were plastered together. Both the nave and the side-aisles were paved with mosaics of which only small patches have so far been found.

Outside each side-aisle, there was an 'external aisle' along the entire length of the building. The external northern aisle was laterally subdivided into various segments. At its western end was a room (no. 3 on Plan) paved with crude white mosaics. In its south-eastern corner the base of a staircase (4) was uncovered. This staircase, supported also by two walls in the northern half of the room, probably enabled access to an upper storey, a terrace or a gallery. This room was probably the ground floor of a small tower from which the sexton called the faithful to prayer by banging on the *simandron* – a wooden board still in use in Greek Orthodox monasteries. From

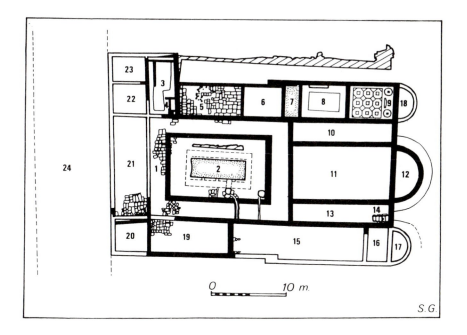

Figure 7.2 Plan of Dor church

1: peristyle court; 2: cistern; 3: tower; 4: staircase; 5: northern vestibule; 6: antechamber; 7: baptismal *piscina*; 8: anointing room; 9: room for celebration of the Eucharist;
10: northern aisle; 11: nave; 12: central apse; 13: southern aisle; 14: saints' tomb; 15:
external southern aisle; 16: room where reliquary column may have stood; 17: southern apse; 18: northern apse; 19: southern vestibule; 20–23: portico; 24: street. The
remains of the podium of the Hellenistic-Roman temple and of a wall belonging to
it are hatched (drawing S. Gibson).

the west, the other segments of the external northern aisle were: an
atrium (5) paved with stone slabs which led into an antechamber
(6), whose plaster floor was originally paved with marble slabs. This
gave access to a shallow, plaster-lined, rectangular basin or baptismal
piscina (7). The eastern and western edges consisted of two steps,

155

each 12 cm high. These areas were followed by two mosaic-paved rooms. The mosaic of room 8 was decorated with sixty red-ochre rose buds – each enclosed in a dark grey calyx – spread out in six north–south rows of ten buds each, on a white ground. At the eastern end of the field a fragmentary *tabula ansata* marked the central axis of the field. The pavement of room 9 combined octagons, squares and stepped lozenges. To the east of this, a stone step probably gave access to a raised area – chancel or altar – now destroyed. Marble screens encased it on its northern and southern faces. The mosaic floor of room 9 extended eastwards on either side of the stone step. Its decorative motif repeated itself symetrically on either side of the step.

The external southern aisle was almost entirely destroyed by the construction of kibbutz houses. Part of the foundations of its eastern apse were uncovered in October 1994, as well as a rectangular room (19) at its western end, paved with stone slabs and corresponding to the atrium in the external northern aisle. The mosaic pavement of the external southern aisle has survived in small patches south of the southern wall of the southern aisle.

To the west, the church was preceded by a stone-paved portico (20–23) fronting the *cardo*, the main north–south street of Byzantine Dora. This is strikingly reminiscent of the *propylea* of the Holy Sepulchre opening onto the Jerusalem *cardo maximus*. The portico of the Dor basilica gave access to a rectangular peristyle court paved with stone slabs (1). Along the east–west axis of the apse and occupying most of the width of the atrium, the floor slabs covered the collapsed vault of a large cistern (figure 7.3). Its plaster lining covered even its pavement of crude white tesserae. Three pairs of corbels or projections protruded from the internal northern and southern faces of the cistern. Water entered through three plaster-lined channels which led from the wall south of the cistern down which gutters probably directed water from the roof. A shaft was cut in the solid rock beside the cistern, plaster-lined and with seven footholds cut into its eastern and western sides. It was linked to the cistern by a doorway cut into the southern wall of the cistern.

At the end of the first season of excavation it was hypothesised that the church had been erected in the fourth century, on the basis of third- and fourth-century coins found in the sandy fill supporting the church. This hypothesis was verified in the 1980 season by the discovery (when lifting the eastern half of the pavement of room 8) of a mosaic pavement with a geometric design, 38 cm below the

Figure 7.3 Cistern (from the north) with water channels, rock-cut shaft, doorway and corbels (photo Z. Radovan).

upper pavement. A bronze *tremessis* coin of Emperor Constantius II (337–61) minted at Cyzicus in Asia Minor was found on the pavement. The building of the first stage of the church must therefore be assigned at the earliest to the first half of the fourth century.

About 2 m to the north of the church, we uncovered the remains of a monumental edifice of late Hellenistic or early Roman date, judging from its masonry, pottery, coins and the leg fragments of a white marble statue. Further traces of this building were located immediately north of the cistern in the peristyle court. The exciting discovery made in November 1994 that the church rested directly on that building confirmed a ten-year-old hunch: the basilica of Dor had been erected over a pagan temple whose *stoa* had been ultimately replaced by the external aisles and by the *atrium* to the west of the cistern, whose *cella* had become the nave and side-aisles of the church and whose *adyton* – the subterranean 'holy of holies' – had been remodelled into a cistern. The plan of the Dor temple would have resembled that of the temple of Nemesis at Rhamnous dating to the sixth century BCE, of the fifth-century Heraion at Argos in mainland Greece, as well as that of the temple of Rhoikos

157

in the sixth-century BCE. Heraion on the island of Samos (Melas 1973: 39–47, 125–31, 179–89; Schoder 1974: 180–1, 190–1). Moreover, the aerial photographs of Dor indicate a grid pattern of streets and buildings to the east of the tell. The temple would have been erected on the south-eastern edge of this area – a characteristic location for Greek cult centres on the edge of the lower city and at the foot of the acropolis (Schoder 1974: 204–5). The temple was burnt, as evidenced by the great quantity of ash overlying the remains of its podium, and its paving stones removed and reused to build the northern wall of the basilica. Thus, the temple of Dor vividly illustrates archaeologically the burning and looting by Christians of the pagan temples of Byzantine Palestine, of which we know historically from the description by Mark the Deacon of the destruction in May 402 of the Marneion of Gaza at the instigation of Porphyry, first bishop of Gaza (Grégoire and Kugener 1930: 55–6).

To the Christian fourth-century basilica of Dor belonged the lower mosaic pavements of rooms 8 and 9, the lower floor of slabs and pebbles of antechamber 5, the lower plaster floors of the *piscina*, of the peristyle court, of the aisles, of the nave, of the apse and of the southern external aisle. The lower pavement of room 8 was burnt at its northern end. Similarly, a fire destroyed the slab and pebble floor of the antechamber. The church was rebuilt on the same plan in the fifth century.

In date and plan, the original basilica of Dor is comparable to the Constantinian foundations of Jerusalem and Bethlehem: the Holy Sepulchre and the Church of the Nativity. One aspect of the Dor basilica, however, appears to be unique. The location of the *piscina* is next to the *atrium* but inside, not outside the ecclesiastical complex. This illustrates the recommendation by the *Testamentum Domini Nostri Jesus Christi*, a canonical law text of the second half of the fifth century, which lays down the rules concerning the plans of churches, that the baptistery should be connected with the *atrium* (Cooper and Maclean 1902: 63). The rhetor Choricius of Gaza describes in the *Laudatio Marciani* how, at the western end of the sixth-century church of St Sergius at Gaza, now destroyed, there was a long portico in the north which included the baptistery (Abel 1931: 16). The tripartite plan of the external northern aisle of the basilica at Dor corresponds to the first three stages of the baptismal liturgy as described in the mid-fourth century *Mystagogical Catecheses* of St Cyril, Bishop of Jerusalem (Piédagnel and Paris 1966).

Figure 7.4 The peristyle court of the Dor basilica from the north-east
(photo Z. Radovan).

Candidates for baptism stood in a vestibule (room 5) called 'the external room' at the western end of the church complex – region of Darkness – and renounced Satan. They then proceeded eastward, towards the divine Light, into 'the internal room' (room 6). There they undressed, were anointed by the bishop, and stepped one by one into the *piscina*. They recited the Act of Faith and were either immersed three times or holy water was poured onto their forehead. Immediately after the baptism they were again anointed by the bishop and then they put on white robes. The third *Catechesis* does not mention a room specially connected with the anointing ceremony, but it is probable that this took place in room 8 at the eastern end of the northern portico, where the newly baptized attended for the first time the celebration of the Eucharist and took communion. The steps leading up to an elevated apse or chancel in room 9 indicate that this room was used for the enactment of the Holy Mysteries.

The external southern aisle of the basilica would have served a different purpose: there as well as in the peristyle court (figure 7.4) sheltered the sick who came to be healed by undergoing a period of *incubatio* – a time of prayer, fasting and often deprivation of sleep.

Figure 7.5 The southern aisle of the Dor basilica with the saints' tomb at its eastern end (after it had been opened), the basin for collecting holy oil north of it, as well as part of the nave and of the central apse (photo Z. Radovan).

The practice of incubation held a prominent place in the rites of divine healing in ancient Greece, for example in the Temple of Asclepios, the God of Medicine, in his sanctuaries at Epidaurus and Pergamon (Simon 1972: 335–6). It was adopted by Christianity and is well attested by saints' 'Lives', notably the seventh-century *Miracles of St Artemios* (Papadopoulos-Kerameus 1905: 1–79). The saint appeared to the sick as they slept in the porticoes of his church at Constantinople and either healed them on the spot or prescribed them a treatment. At Dor, the sick gathered round the remains of two saints, whose names are not known, but whose tomb was found in the eastern end of the southern aisle (figure 7.5). The tomb was closed by five slabs placed crosswise in a row oriented east–west. A small hole, 16–18 cm in diameter, had been cut in the centre of the western edge of the easternmost slab. The hole was lined with an earthenware pipe. We suspect that oil would have been poured into the tomb through this pipe in order to be sanctified by contact with the remains of the saint. The oil would have drained into a plaster-lined basin 2 m long and 1.4 m wide, between the tomb and the northern wall of the southern aisle, then to be used for healing the sick. This interpretation was confirmed by the discovery of oily deposits around the lower portions of the eastern wall of the southern aisle. In Syria, the bones of saints were generally held in stone reli-quaries, coffers in the shape of small sarcophagi. Oil was poured into a hole pierced in the cover slab and, once sanctified by contact with the relics, drained out through another hole at the bottom of the coffer (Lassus 1947: 163–7). The reliquary-tomb of Dor is the first of its kind to have been found in Palestine.

Holy oil collected at the tombs of saints was carried back home by pilgrims in *eulogiae* or *ampullae*, small moulded pottery or embossed metal flasks bearing representations of the holy places where the oil had been sanctified. The most famous examples are thirty-six silver *ampullae* in the treasury of the cathedrals of Bobbio and Monza in Northern Italy, on which were depicted the Bethlehem grotto, the Cross of Calvary and the Anastasis (Grabar 1958).

Both theologians and pilgrims believed that holy oil ensured protection from the temptations of the Devil, one of the chief of which was drunkenness. St John Chrysostom advocated pilgims to:

> Take holy oil and anoint all your body, your tongue, your lips, your neck, your eyes, and nevermore will you fall victim to drunkenness. For the oil, by its perfume, reminds you of the struggles of the martyrs, restrains licentiousness, strengthens steadfastness, and puts an end to the illnesses of the soul.
>
> (*In Martyres Homilia*, 665)

The Byzantine centuries were an age of relic-hunting. Pilgrims high and low fought over holy relics to such an extent that Egeria tells of an eager pilgrim, who when kissing the wooden relics of the True Cross in the Holy Sepulchre, actually bit off a fragment and made off with it in his teeth (*Itinerarium Egeriae* 37; Pétré 1948: 234–5). It is no surprise therefore that pilgrims visited Dor. Not only was there a saints' tomb to pray at, but Dor could pride itself on possessing a memorial of Christ's death. In the 1952 excavations, about 100 m east of the basilica, a grey marble column was found lying on the surface. A three-line Greek inscription ('A stone of the Holy Golgotha') had been carved 92 cm above its base. Beneath the inscription there was a hollow cross. A small cross had been carved at each of the four ends of the central cross. The hollow probably contained a fragment of the Golgotha, the rock of Calvary, enclosed in a cross-shaped metal reliquary, riveted into the column – for there were holes at the end of each branch of the central cross (Leibovitch

1953). Such a prized relic must have exercised tremendous magnetism over pilgrims travelling from the north along the *Via Maris*, or disembarking at the port of Dora, whence they could ascend directly to the church.

This port consisted of a double harbour, facing north and south, one on each side of the ancient tell, with two basins ensuring protection against winds from all directions. Dora offered suitable landing facilities along an almost harbourless coast. Its role as major port and road junction on the trade and pilgrim routes linking Egypt and North Africa to the Syro-Cilician hinterland, is underlined by the quantity and variety of imported pottery found in the course of the excavation of the basilica There were Egyptian white storage jars, 'Late Roman C' and 'North African Red Slip' bowls and plates, as well as storage jars from Asia Minor.

To cope with the crowds of pilgrims and worshippers, it was necessary to include in the planning of the Dor basilica, as in the Constantinian foundations of Jerusalem and Bethlehem, an extra-large courtyard with an impressive cistern. Although fresh-water wells were abundant in the region of Dor, storage without the risk of evaporation was necessary to maintain a constant supply of water for the church, the episcopal staff, the pilgrims and the sick.

The final fate of the basilica of Dor is clearly imprinted on the remains. Dor was destroyed by fire, as evidenced by an ashy layer and collapsed material: chunks of wall plaster, marble fragments, broken storage jars, glass window panes, glass chandeliers or *polycandela* hanging from bronze chains and hooks, all mixed with iron nails, door-latches and a fragmentary lead *polycandelon* molten by fire. Unlike most destructions of Byzantine ecclesiastical sites in Palestine, this destruction can be dated neither to the Persian invasion of 613–14 nor to the Moslem conquest of 636. At the Council of the Lateran in 649, Bishop Stephen of Dora appeared before Pope Martin and was introduced as 'first of the church council of Jerusalem'. His role as vicar of the see of Jerusalem was to institute bishops, presbyters and deacons as long as there was no possibility of appointing a patriarch in Jerusalem owing to the Arab take-over. Stephen deputised for the Jerusalem patriarchate, which had fallen vacant at Sophronius I's death in 645, both because of the pre-eminence of his own see of Dora, first suffragant of the metropolis of Caesarea which was in the hands of the Arabs since 640, and as legate of Pope Theodorus, Martin's predecessor. The patriarchal line in Jerusalem was restored only in 705. Owing to ecclesiastical

Figure 7.6 The mosaic pavement of room 9 in the external northern aisle damaged by Ottoman graves oriented towards Mecca (photo Z. Radovan).

intrigues, Pope Martin transferred his delegation of authority from Stephen of Dor to John of Philadelphia, modern Amman in Transjordan. Following this move in 649, nothing further is known of Byzantine Dora. However, the pottery in the destruction level at Dora appears to indicate a late eighth-century or ninth-century date. Under the Abbassids, the Christians of Palestine became the victims of an intolerant Islam. The burning of the episcopal basilica of Dor fits perhaps in this context, but could also have been purely accidental.

Between the fifteenth and eighteenth centuries, the basilica of Dor was used as a cemetery by the Arab population of neighbouring Tanturah. Tombs were dug into the upper mosaic pavement of the external northern aisle (figure 7.6), north of it and at the eastern end of the church. We have uncovered 120 tombs spread over five *strata* and arranged in family groups. The skeletal material has provided us with important anthropological data on the Arab population of Palestine under Ottoman rule.[3] In the late eighteenth century, a 'new' cemetery was established further south, and the site of the basilica of Dor gradually became an overgrown mound.

NOTES

1 We are grateful to Dr E. D. Hunt of the Department of Classics, University of Durham, for discussing with us at length the importance of the basilica of Dor within the wider context of Byzantine Pilgrimage to the Holy Land.

2 So far, four seasons of excavations have been conducted on behalf of the Israel Department of Antiquities in June and July 1979 and 1980, and jointly on behalf of both the Israel Antiquities Authority and the French Centre National de la Recherche Scientifique in October 1983 and October–November 1994. The 1983 and 1994 seasons were also both funded by the Russell Trust, Scotland and by Somerville College, Oxford (Katharine and Leonard Woolley Fellowship Fund), the 1983 season by the European Science Foundation, and the 1994 season by the French Ministry of Foreign Affairs, the Centre de Recherche Français de Jérusalem and the Dominican Ecole Biblique et Archéologique Française de Jérusalem. To these institutions we are heavily indebted for providing excavation permits, financial or technical support. Thanks are also due to Mr K. Raveh, formerly Director of the Center of Nautical and Regional Archaeology, Dor, for his invaluable help since he first introduced us to the site of the Dor basilica in the winter of 1979. All the photographs are reproduced by courtesy of the Israel Antiquities Authority. The plan of the Dor Church complex was drawn by Dr S. Gibson of the Palestine Exploration Fund, London, on the basis of excavations plans by Mr I. Vatkin of the Israel Antiquities Authority and by M. D. Ladiray of the Centre de Recherche Français de Jérusalem. We wish to thank them here for their detailed surveying work and architectural analyses.

3 The Ottoman skeletal material as well as the remains of the two Byzantine saints have been studied by Professor P. Smith of the Hadassah Medical School, Hebrew University of Jerusalem. The numismatic evidence from the Ottoman graves was examined by Mr A. Berman of the Israel Antiquities Authority. We are grateful to them both for their co-operation.

BIBLIOGRAPHY

Abel, F.-M. (1931) 'Gaza au VIᵉ siècle d'après le rhéteur Chorikios', *RB* 40: 14–27.
Avi-Yonah, M. (1954) *The Madaba Mosaic Map*, Jerusalem: Israel Exploration Society.
Cooper, J. and Maclean, A. J. (eds) (1902) *The Testament of Our Lord*, Edinburgh: Blackwood.
Egeria, *Itinerarium Egeriae*, ed. H. Pétré (1948) *Ethérie. Journal de Voyage* (*Sources Chrétiennes* 21), Paris: Cerf.
Gibson, S. and Taylor, J. E. (1994) *Beneath the Church of the Holy Sepulchre: Jerusalem. The archaeology and early history of traditional Golgotha*, PEF Monograph Series Major 1, London.
Grabar, A. (1958) *Ampoules de Terre Sainte*, Paris: C. Klinksieck.

Grégoire, H. and Kugener, M.–A. (eds) (1930) *Marc le Diacre, Vie de Porphyre Evêque de Gaza*, Paris: Les Belles Lettres.

Hunt, E. D. (1982) *Holy Land Pilgrimage in the Later Roman Empire AD 312–460*, Oxford: Clarendon Press.

Jerome, *Onomastikon*, ed. E. Klostermann (1904, reprinted 1966), Leipzig–Berlin: Georg Olms Verlag.

John Chrysostom (St) *In Martyres Homilia*, ed. J.-P. Migne, *PG* 50: 661–6.

Klostermann, E. (ed.) (1904) *Eusebius. Das Onomastikon der Biblischen Ortsnamen*, Leipzig and Berlin; reprinted 1966, Hildesheim: Georg Olms Verlag.

Lassus, J. (1947) *Sanctuaires Chrétiens de Syrie*, Paris: P. Geuthner.

Leibovitch, J. (1953) 'The reliquary column of Dor', *Christian News in Israel* 5, 22–3.

Melas, E. (ed.) (1973) *Temples and Sanctuaries of Ancient Greece*, London: Thames and Hudson.

Migne, J.-B. (ed.) (1857–1912) *Patrologiae Graecae cursus completus, Series graeca (PG)*, Paris: J.-P. Migne.

Papadopoulos-Kerameus, A. (ed.) (1905) *Diegesis ton Thaumaton tou Agious Megalomartyriou Artemiou (Varia Graeca Sacra)*, St Petersburg: Tip. V. F. Kirsbauma.

Pétré, H. (ed.) (1948) *Ethérie. Journal de Voyage (Sources Chrétiennes* 21), Paris: Cerf.

Piédagnel, A. and Paris, P. (eds) (1966) *Cyrille de Jérusalem: Catéchèses Mystagogiques (Sources Chrétiennes* 126), Paris: Cerf.

Pliny the Elder, *Naturalis Historia*, ed. H. Rackam, London, 1947–63, Loeb Classical Library, London: Heinemann; Cambridge, Mass.: Harvard University Press.

Schoder, R. V. (1974) *Ancient Greece from the Air*, London: Thames and Hudson.

Simon, M. (1972) *La Civilisation de l'Antiquité et le Christianisme*, Paris: Arthaud.

Wilkinson, J. (1977) *Jerusalem Pilgrims before the Crusades*, Jerusalem: Ariel.

INDEX OF AUTHORS

INDEX OF PLACES

INDEX OF PLACES

GENERAL INDEX

ethnicity 42, 43
Eudocia (empress) 148
eulogiae 161
Exodus 5, 7, 8, 22, 45, 48
Ezekiel 41

First Jewish Revolt 98, 130, 136

Genesis Apocryphon (1QGenAp) 72, 82
Gentile mission 121–2
grain ships 149

Habakkuk Commentary (1QpHab) 72, 82
habiru 5.24, 40, 55
Hadad (deity) 137
Hadrian (emperor) 146, 148, 152
haggadah 48
Hasmonaeans 133–6
Hebrew language 45
Helena (empress) 3, 147
Helena of Adiabene 5
Hellenism, Hellenisation 129–31, 136
Hellenistic period 134–6
Herod Antipas 127, 129, 136
Herod Archelaus 81, 82, 90
Herod the Great 81, 82, 90, 98, 99, 127,
   134, 136, 145
Hezekiah, king of Judah 65, 74
Hilarion (calligrapher) 150
historical Jesus 117–44
History of Religions School 132
history 20, 21, 45–8
Hittites 6, 41
house of Joseph 46, 47
Hurrians 43
Hymn Scroll (1QH) 72, 82
Hyrcanus I 83, 90
Hyrcanus II 81

incubatio 159, 160
inkwells 88, 91
Innocentius 151
inscriptions 32, 34, 52, 56, 61, 63, 110,
   128, 136, 161
Iron Age 25–8, 30, 43, 60
Isaiah Scrolls (1QIs.a, b) 72
Israel Department of Antiquities and
   Museums (Israel Antiquities Authority)
   153
Israel Exploration Society 5, 98, 99
Israelite religion 51–66
Israelites 43, 44
Itinerarium Egeriae 161
Ituraeans 133–5

James, brother of Jesus 146
Jannaeus, king Alexander 81, 82
Jehoash, king of Israel 62

Jehoiachin, king of Judah 11
Jehoshaphat, king of Judah 74
Jehu, king of Israel 11
Jesus xii, 11, 117–38
Jethro (Midianite) 47
Jewish Revolt 132–5 CE 90
John Hyrcanus 81
John of Gischala 110
Jonathan (Maccabee) 91
Jonathan (son of Saul) 60
Jordanian Department of Antiquities 72,
   73
Joshua 20, 152
Joshua, book of 22, 27
Josiah, king of Judah 65
Judas the Galilaean 123
Judges 22
Judges, book of 27
Jupiter Capitolinus 146
Justus of Tiberias 128

Last Supper 146
Late Bronze Age 24–6, 27, 28, 30, 33,
   40, 41, 43, 55, 60
linen 89
Luke's Gospel 127

mansio 150, 151
Manual of Discipline (*see* Community
   Rule)
Mark the Deacon 158
Mark's Gospel 121, 122, 127, 130
Martin (pope) 162, 163
Mattathias, king of Judah 81
Mayflower 47
Melania the Younger 151
Melchizedek Midrash (11QMelch) 73
Meribaal 60
Merneptah 22, 43
Mesha stele 10, 11
miqva'oth 10, 84, 101, 123, 130, 135,
   136
Mishnah 99, 105, 125
mishpahah 27
mono-Yahwism 53, 55
monolatry 52, 53, 64
monotheism 51, 64
Moses 45, 47, 54, 56, 57, 145
Moslem conquest 162
Mystagogical Catacheses 158, 159

Nahum Commentary (4QpNah) 82
Napoleon 3, 5
Nebuchadnezzar 145
Negebite ware 29
Neolithic period 8, 9
Nero (emperor) 81, 124, 129
nomadism, nomads 24, 33

INDEX OF REFERENCES
TO BIBLICAL TEXTS AND
WORKS OF JOSEPHUS